Aging Issues, Health and Financial Alternatives

# The Older Americans Act: Provisions, Funding and Programs

Jamie N. Palamino
Editor

Nova Science Publishers, Inc.
*New York*

Copyright ©2011 by Nova Science Publishers, Inc.

**All rights reserved.** No part of this book may be reproduced, stored in a retrieval system or transmitted in any form or by any means: electronic, electrostatic, magnetic, tape, mechanical photocopying, recording or otherwise without the written permission of the Publisher.

For permission to use material from this book please contact us:
Telephone 631-231-7269; Fax 631-231-8175
Web Site: http://www.novapublishers.com

## NOTICE TO THE READER

The Publisher has taken reasonable care in the preparation of this book, but makes no expressed or implied warranty of any kind and assumes no responsibility for any errors or omissions. No liability is assumed for incidental or consequential damages in connection with or arising out of information contained in this book. The Publisher shall not be liable for any special, consequential, or exemplary damages resulting, in whole or in part, from the readers' use of, or reliance upon, this material. Any parts of this book based on government reports are so indicated and copyright is claimed for those parts to the extent applicable to compilations of such works.

Independent verification should be sought for any data, advice or recommendations contained in this book. In addition, no responsibility is assumed by the publisher for any injury and/or damage to persons or property arising from any methods, products, instructions, ideas or otherwise contained in this publication.

This publication is designed to provide accurate and authoritative information with regard to the subject matter covered herein. It is sold with the clear understanding that the Publisher is not engaged in rendering legal or any other professional services. If legal or any other expert assistance is required, the services of a competent person should be sought. FROM A DECLARATION OF PARTICIPANTS JOINTLY ADOPTED BY A COMMITTEE OF THE AMERICAN BAR ASSOCIATION AND A COMMITTEE OF PUBLISHERS.

Additional color graphics may be available in the e-book version of this book.

LIBRARY OF CONGRESS CATALOGING-IN-PUBLICATION DATA

The Older Americans Act : provisions, funding, and programs / editor, Jamie N. Palamino.
   p. cm.
 Includes index.
 Includes reprints of legislative branch publications.
 ISBN 978-1-61122-801-4 (softcover)
 1. United States. Older Americans Act of 1965. 2. Older people--Services for--United States. 3. Old age assistance--Law and legislation--United States. I. Palamino, Jamie N. II. Colello, Kirsten J. III. United States. Congress. Senate. Special Committee on Aging.
 KF3737.A25 2010
 344.7303'26--dc22
                     2010042629

*Published by Nova Science Publishers, Inc. ✝ New York*

# CONTENTS

| | | |
|---|---|---|
| **Preface** | | vii |
| **Chapter 1** | Older Americans Act: Funding<br>*Angela Napili and Kirsten J. Colello* | 1 |
| **Chapter 2** | Older Americans Act: Title III Nutrition Services Program<br>*Kirsten J. Colello* | 35 |
| **Chapter 3** | Older Americans Act: Preliminary Observations on Services Requested by Seniors and Challenges in Providing Assistance<br>*Kay E. Brown* | 47 |
| **Chapter 4** | Testimony of Paul Downey, President, National Association of Nutrition and Aging Serviced Program (NANASP), before the Senate Special Committee on Aging Hearing, "2011 Reauthorization of the Older Americans Act" | 65 |
| **Chapter 5** | Testimony of Kathy Greenle, Assistant Secretary for Aging, U.S. Department of Health and Human Services, before the Senate Special Committee on Aging Hearing, "2011 Reauthorization of the Older Americans Act" | 69 |

| | | |
|---|---|---|
| **Chapter 6** | Older Americans Act: Long-Term Care Ombudsman Program<br>*Kirsten J. Colello* | **75** |
| **Chapter Sources** | | **87** |
| **Index** | | **89** |

# PREFACE

The Older Americans Act (OAA) is the major federal vehicle for the delivery of social and nutritional services for older persons. These include supportive services, congregate nutritional services (meals served at group sites such as senior centers, community centers, schools, churches, or senior housing complexes), home-delivered nutritional services, family caregiver support, community service employment, the long-term care ombudsman program, and services to prevent the abuse, neglect and exploitation of older persons. This book provides an overview of the services and issues of the Older Americans Act and provides information about legislation which would increase authorizations or funding to certain OAA programs.

Chapter 1- The Older Americans Act (OAA) is the major federal vehicle for the delivery of social and nutrition services for older persons. These include supportive services, congregate nutrition services (meals served at group sites such as senior centers, community centers, schools, churches, or senior housing complexes), home-delivered nutrition services, family caregiver support, community service employment, the long-term care ombudsman program, and services to prevent the abuse, neglect and exploitation of older persons. The OAA also supports grants to older Native Americans and research, training, and demonstration activities. Funding for most OAA programs is provided through appropriations legislation for the Departments of Labor, Health and Human Services, Education, and Related Agencies (Labor-HHS-Education).

Chapter 2- The elderly nutrition services program, authorized under Title III of the Older Americans Act, provides grants to state agencies on aging to support congregate and home-delivered meals for people aged 60 and older.

The program is designed to address problems of food insecurity, promote socialization, and promote the health and well-being of older persons through nutrition and nutrition-related services. It is the largest Older Americans Act program, funded at $819.5 million in FY2010, accounting for over one-third (35%) of the Act's total funding. In FY2008, the most recent year for which data are available, over 240 million meals were served to about 2.6 million people; 61% were served to frail older people living at home, and 39% were served in congregate settings. The number of home-delivered meals served has outpaced congregate meals, growing by almost 44% from FY1990 to FY2008; the number of congregate meals served declined by 34%. The faster growth in home-delivered meals is partially due to relatively higher growth in federal funding for home-delivered meals over that time period, as well as state decisions to focus funds on frail older people living at home. Congress approved the Older Americans Act Amendments of 2006 (P.L. 109-365) extending the Act's authorization of appropriations through FY2011.

Chapter 3- Administered by the Administration on Aging (AoA) in the Department of Health and Human Services (HHS), Title III of the Older Americans Act (OAA) is intended to assist individuals age 60 and older by providing supportive services. Title III, Medicaid and Medicare, state, and other sources of funding provide for several types of services, including congregate and home-delivered meals, transportation, and support for caregivers.

Chapter 4 – This is a statement of Paul Downey, President, National Association of Nutrition and Aging Services Programs, before Senate Special Committee on Aging Hearing-2011 Reauthorization of the Older Americans Act.

Chapter 5 – This is a statement of Kathy Greenlee, Assistant Secretary for Aging, United States Department of Health and Human Services, before the Senate Special Committee on Aging Field Hearing on Reauthorization of the Older Americans Act.

Chapter 6- The purpose of the Long-Term Care Ombudsman Program is to investigate and resolve complaints made by, or on behalf of, older persons who are residents of long-term care facilities. Established under Title VII of the Older Americans Act (OAA), the Administration on Aging (AoA) within the Department of Health and Human Services (HHS) administers the nationwide program. As of 2007, there are 53 state Long-Term Care Ombudsman Programs operating in all 50 states, the District of Columbia, Guam, and Puerto Rico, and 569 local programs. The program is funded by two separate titles of the OAA, in addition to other federal sources, state funds, and nonfederal funds. With respect to staffing, the program receives significant support from volunteers. In FY2007, over 1,300 paid staff and 12,600 volunteers investigated more than 282,000 resident complaints. Issues regarding residents' care were the chief complaint in nursing homes, followed by residents' rights issues in FY2007. Among residents in other long-term care facilities, the top complaint categories were quality of life and residents' rights.

In: The Older Americans Act: Provisions,... ISBN: 978-1-61122-801-4
Editor: Jamie N. Palamino ©2011 Nova Science Publishers, Inc.

*Chapter 1*

# OLDER AMERICANS ACT: FUNDING

## *Angela Napili and Kirsten J. Colello*

### SUMMARY

The Older Americans Act (OAA) is the major federal vehicle for the delivery of social and nutrition services for older persons. These include supportive services, congregate nutrition services (meals served at group sites such as senior centers, community centers, schools, churches, or senior housing complexes), home-delivered nutrition services, family caregiver support, community service employment, the long-term care ombudsman program, and services to prevent the abuse, neglect and exploitation of older persons. The OAA also supports grants to older Native Americans and research, training, and demonstration activities. Funding for most OAA programs is provided through appropriations legislation for the Departments of Labor, Health and Human Services, Education, and Related Agencies (Labor-HHS-Education).

The FY2010 Consolidated Appropriations Act (P.L. 111-117), signed into law December 16, 2009, provides $2.328 billion for OAA programs in FY2010.

The FY2009 Omnibus Appropriations Act (P.L. 111-8) provided $2.052 billion for OAA programs for FY2009. The American Recovery and Reinvestment Act of 2009 (ARRA, P.L. 111- 5) provided $220.0 million in additional FY2009 funding ($100.0 million for nutrition programs and $120.0

million for the Title V, Community Service Employment for Older Americans Program, or CSEOA). Total FY2009 OAA funding was $2.272 billion.

The FY2010 funding level for OAA programs is a 13% increase over the funding provided by the FY2009 Omnibus Appropriations Act, and a 2% increase over total FY2009 funding (including both the Omnibus and ARRA). CSEOA received the bulk of this increased funding. Congress appropriated $825.4 million to CSEOA in FY2010, compared with $691.9 million in FY2009 funding ($571.9 million from the FY2009 Omnibus, and $120.0 million from ARRA).

The President's FY2011 Budget proposes $2.209 billion for OAA programs, 5% less than the FY2010 level. CSEOA would receive $600.425 million, 27% less than its FY2010 level.

The FY2011 Budget proposes a $102.5 million Caregiver Initiative that would increase funding for services to help family caregivers. The Caregiver Initiative proposes a $48.0 million increase for supportive services and a $48.0 million increase for family caregiver support services, both under OAA's Title III. The Caregiver Initiative also proposes a $2.0 million increase for Native American supportive services and a $2.0 million increase for Native American caregiver support services, both under Title VI. Finally, the Caregiver Initiative proposes a $2.5 million increase for Lifespan Respite Care.

On March 23, 2010, President Obama signed into law a comprehensive health care reform bill, the Patient Protection and Affordable Care Act (PPACA; P.L. 111-148). Among other things, the act appropriates $10 million in mandatory spending for Aging and Disability Resource Centers (ADRCs) through FY2014. It also authorizes additional funding to the aging network, including $15.0 million to ADRCs and $10.0 million to Area Agencies on Aging (AAAs) for outreach and education programs related to Medicare low-income assistance programs. These funds are available for obligation through FY2012.

This report provides details of FY2010 funding and the FY2011 budget request for OAA as well as for programs such as the Alzheimer's Disease Supportive Services Program (ADSSP) and Lifespan Respite Care Program which are administered by the Administration on Aging (AOA), but authorized under the Public Health Service Act (PHSA).

## INTRODUCTION

Originally enacted in 1965, the Older Americans Act (OAA) supports a wide range of social services and programs for older persons.[1] These include supportive services, congregate nutrition services (meals served at group sites such as senior centers, community centers, schools, churches, or senior housing complexes), home-delivered nutrition services, family caregiver support, community service employment, the long-term care ombudsman program, and services to prevent the abuse, neglect, and exploitation of older persons. Except for Title V, Community Service Employment for Older Americans, all programs are administered by the Administration on Aging (AOA) in the Department of Health and Human Services (HHS). Title V is administered by the Department of Labor (DOL) Employment and Training Administration.

Funding for most OAA programs is provided through appropriations legislation for the Departments of Labor, Health and Human Services, Education and Related Agencies (LaborHHS-ED). Funds for most AOA programs (Titles II, III, IV, VI, and VII) are part of the HHS appropriations; Title V is part of the DOL appropriations. In FY2003, Congress transferred administrative authority for the nutrition services incentive grant program from the U.S. Department of Agriculture (USDA), where it had been since its inception, to AOA. The program retains a separate authorization of appropriations under Title III and its appropriations are part of the Labor-HHS-ED appropriations legislation.

The following report provides details of FY2010 funding and the FY2011 budget request for OAA. It then discusses FY2010 funding and the FY2011 budget request for programs administered by AOA, but authorized under the Public Health Service Act (PHSA). Finally, it provides information about legislation that has been considered in the 111th Congress which would increase authorizations or funding to certain OAA programs.

The appendixes provide more detailed funding information. Table A-1 of Appendix A provides funding levels for OAA programs from FY2003 through FY2010. Table A-1 also includes appropriations for the 2005 White House Conference on Aging, which was authorized by the Older Americans Act Amendments of 2000 (P.L. 106-501). Finally, the table includes appropriations for two programs administered by the AOA and authorized by the Public Health Service Act (PHSA): Alzheimer's Disease Supportive Services Program and the Lifespan Respite Care program. Table B-1 of Appendix B compares the programs' FY2010 funding levels to the President's

FY2011 Budget proposal. Table C-1 of Appendix C shows the authorization of appropriations for each title of the act as stipulated by the 2006 Older Americans Act Amendments (P.L. 109-365). Appendix D provides information about OAA's historical development, including a summary of major amendments to the act.

## FY2010 FUNDING AND FY2011 BUDGET REQUEST

The FY2010 Consolidated Appropriations Act (P.L. 111-117), signed into law December 16, 2009, provides $2.328 billion for OAA programs in FY2010. **Figure 1** shows the distribution of FY2010 OAA funding by program. Title III State and Community Programs on Aging received the largest proportion of FY2010 funding under the act with 59% of funding appropriated to nutrition, supportive services, family caregivers, and health promotion activities. More than one-third (35%) of OAA funding in FY2010 was allocated to Title V, the Community Service Employment for Older Americans Program (CSEOA). The remainder of FY2010 OAA funding was allocated to AOA activities under Title II (2.8%), grants to Native Americans under Title VI (1.5%), vulnerable elder rights protection activities under Title VII (0.9%), and research, training, and demonstration activities under Title IV (0.8%).

The FY2009 Omnibus Appropriations Act (P.L. 111-8) provided $2.052 billion for OAA programs for FY2009. The American Recovery and Reinvestment Act of 2009 (ARRA; P.L. 111-5), provided $220 million in additional FY2009 funding ($100 million for nutrition programs and $120 million for the Title V Senior Community Service Employment for Older Americans). Total FY2009 OAA funding was $2.272 billion.

The FY2010 funding level for OAA programs is a 13% increase over the funding provided by the FY2009 Omnibus Appropriations Act, and a 2% increase over total FY2009 funding (including both the Omnibus and ARRA).

On February 1, 2010, the President released the FY2011 Budget. It proposes $2.209 billion for OAA programs, 5% less than the FY2010 level. CSEOA would receive $600.425 million, 27% less than its FY2010 level.

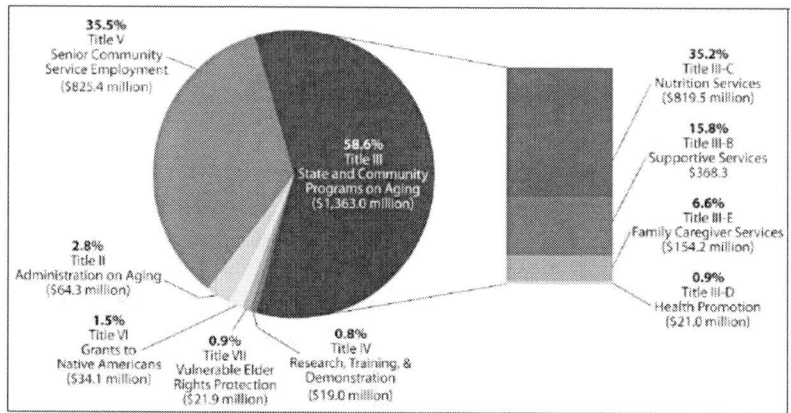

Source: Prepared by CRS based on H.Rept. 111-366, *Conference Report to Accompany H.R. 3288*, pp. 989, 1298-1299; Administration on Aging, *FY2010 Appropriation*, http://www.aoa.gov/AoARoot/About/Budget/docs/ Appropriation_FY_2010.pdf.

Notes: Sums may total to more than 100% due to rounding. Does not include other programs administered by AOA such as Lifespan Respite Care or Alzheimer's Disease Supportive Services Program.

Figure 1. Older Americans Act, FY2010 Funding (percentage of total OAA funding, which is $2.328 billion)

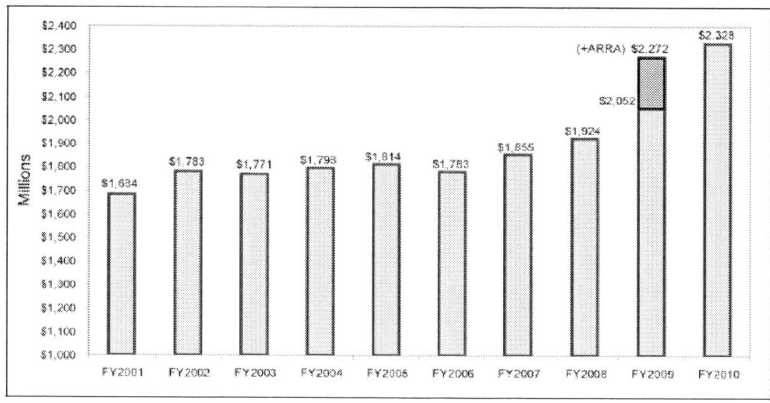

Source: Prepared by CRS based on appropriations legislation and committee reports.

Note: ARRA is the American Recovery and Reinvestment Act (P.L. 111-5), which provided $220 million to Older Americans Act programs in FY2009 in addition to the $2,052 million provided by the FY2009 Omnibus Appropriations Act (P.L. 111-8).

Figure 2. Funding for Older Americans Act Programs, FY2001-FY2010

The FY2011 Budget includes a $102.5 million Caregiver Initiative that would increase funds for AOA services to help families with elder care and caregiving responsibilities. This request includes a $48.0 million increase for supportive services under OAA's Title III-B, a $48.0 million increase for family caregiver support services under Title III-E, a $2.0 million increase for Native American supportive services under Title VI, a $2.0 million increase for Native American caregiver support services under Title VI-C, and a $2.5 million increase for Lifespan Respite Care (which is authorized by PHSA).

The following provides details of FY2010 funding and the FY2011 Budget Request under Titles II through VII of the OAA. Title I (Declaration of Objectives) does not authorize appropriations.

## Title II. Administration on Aging

Title II establishes AOA within HHS as the chief federal agency advocate for older persons and sets out the responsibilities of AOA and the Assistant Secretary for Aging. The Assistant Secretary is appointed by the President with the advice and consent of the Senate.

Funding authorized under Title II goes toward program administration and Aging Network support activities. Aging Network support activities currently include the following:

- *National Eldercare Locator*, a nationwide toll-free phone number and website that helps identify community resources for older persons[2];
- *Pension Counseling and Information Program* funds six regional counseling projects that help older Americans learn about and receive the retirement benefits to which they are entitled;
- *Senior Medicare Patrol Program* funds projects that educate older Americans and their families to recognize and report Medicare and Medicaid fraud;
- *National Long-Term Care Ombudsman Resource Center* provides training and technical assistance to state and local long-term care ombudsmen;
- *National Center on Elder Abuse* provides information to the public and professionals, and provides training and technical assistance to state elder abuse agencies and to community-based organizations;

- *National Center for Benefits Outreach and Enrollment* helps to enroll seniors and persons with disabilities into federal and state benefits programs for which they are eligible but not yet enrolled[3]; and
- *Health and Long-Term Care Programs Initiative* (formerly "Choices for Independence") helps older Americans plan for long-term care services and supports so that they can maintain their independence in the community.[4]

The FY2010 Consolidated Appropriations Act (P.L. 111-117) provides $64.3 million for Title II in FY2010, a 6% increase over the FY2009 funding level. Of this amount, $30.6 million are for the Health and Long-Term Care Programs Initiative, which reflects provisions newly authorized in the Older American Act Amendments of 2006 (P.L. 109-365). Specifically, this initiative builds on existing AOA programs related to Aging and Disability Resource Centers (ADRCs), Evidence- Based Disease Prevention, and Nursing Home Diversion/Community Living Programs.

As described by AOA, Health and Long-Term Care Programs focus on "empowering older individuals to remain healthy and independent for as long as possible and on breaking the cycle of unnecessary admissions and readmissions for costly nursing home care and hospital services."[5] The initiative has three components:

*First*, Aging and Disability Resource Centers provide "one-stop shop/single-entry points" for consumer information on all long-term care options. ADRCs provide information and access to community-based services to help older individuals to continue to live at home. There are currently more than 200 ADRC sites nationwide, operating in 49 states, three territories, and the District of Columbia.[6]

*Second*, "Evidence-Based Disease Prevention" programs help seniors change behavior to reduce risk of disease and disability. Funds support activities in areas such as falls prevention, physical activity, and chronic disease self-management. This component builds on existing Title IV evidence-based disease prevention projects.

*Third*, the "Nursing Home Diversion/Community Living Programs" component gives states funds they could use to help seniors avoid institutionalization. It targets low-to-moderate-income individuals who are at risk of nursing home placement but who are not yet eligible for Medicaid. This component uses ADRCs to identify these individuals, to help them develop care plans, and to link them to needed services.[7] This component emphasizes "flexible, consumer-directed models, such as Cash and Counseling."[8]

The FY2011 Budget requests $36.2 million for Title II, a $28.0 million decrease from the FY2010 level. This decrease appears to be reflected in a proposed increase in funding Health and Long- Term Care Programs under the authority of Title IV, which funds training, research, and demonstration projects, rather than as part of Aging Network Support Activities under Title II. The Budget Justification explains "Health and Long-Term Care funding allows AOA to identify and evaluate the best models and practices nationwide, as part of its overall strategy for strengthening its core programs and the national aging services network. To this end, AOA draws on the latest research and the results of evaluations of its core programs at the State and local level to identify cutting edge, state-of-the-art approaches for further testing and replication."[9]

HHS has also announced that a separate funding stream of $32.5 million of ARRA money would be provided to AOA for evidence-based chronic disease self-management programs (CDSMPs) for older people.[10] $27.0 million will be used for cooperative agreements with State Units on Aging and State Departments of Health to deploy CDSMPs. These cooperative agreements will be administered by AOA. The initiative builds on AOA's existing Evidence-Based Disease Prevention Programs.[11] AOA's CDSMP activities will also receive $2.5 million for an interagency agreement with the Centers for Medicare and Medicaid Services to develop a quality assurance program, and $3.0 million to continue funding a National Technical Assistance Center on Evidence-Based Prevention Programs.[12]

On March 23, 2010, President Obama signed into law a comprehensive health care reform bill, the Patient Protection and Affordable Care Act (PPACA; P.L. 111-148). The act contains provisions that would provide additional funding for Aging and Disability Resource Centers (ADRCs), AAAs, and the National Center for Benefits and Outreach Enrollment. Specifically, Section 2405 of PPACA appropriates $10.0 million in mandatory spending for ADRCs for each of FY2010 through FY2014. Additionally, Section 3306 of PPACA provides $45.0 million for outreach and education programs related to Medicare low-income assistance programs. Of the $45.0 million, $15.0 million is allocated to AAAs, $10.0 million allocated to ADRCs, and $5.0 million allocated to the National Center for Benefits and Outreach Enrollment.[13] These funds are available for obligation through FY2012. The HHS Secretary is authorized to enlist the support of these entities to conduct outreach activities aimed at preventing disease and promoting wellness as an additional use of these funds.

## Title III. Grants for State and Community Programs on Aging

The major program under the OAA, Title III—Grants for State and Community Programs on Aging—authorizes grants to 56 State and 629 Area Agencies on Aging to act as advocates on behalf of, and to coordinate programs for older persons.[14] Title III accounts for 59% of the OAA's total FY2010 funding. States receive separate allotments of funds for supportive services and centers, family caregiver support, congregate nutrition (meals served at group sites such as senior centers, community centers, schools, churches, or senior housing complexes), home-delivered nutrition services, the nutrition services incentive grant program (allotted to states based on each state's share of total meals served nationwide by the nutrition services program the previous year), and disease prevention and health promotion services.[15] In FY2008, almost 10 million older persons were served by Title III programs.[16]

The FY2010 Consolidated Appropriations Act (P.L. 111-117) provides $1.363 billion for Title III. This is a 1% increase over the $1.346 billion provided by the FY2009 Omnibus Appropriations Act (P.L. 111-8), and a 6% decrease from the total FY2009 funding level (including both the Omnibus and the American Recovery and Reinvestment Act). Together, the FY2009 Omnibus and ARRA had provided $1.443 billion for Title III in FY2009.

ARRA provided $65 million for congregate meals and $32 million for home-delivered meals in FY2009.[17] AOA obligated all of these ARRA funds in FY2009. As of early February 2010, states had spent 40% of funding, and they are anticipated to spend the rest by the end of FY2010, according to AOA.[18] In reports accompanying earlier versions of the bill, the House and Senate Appropriations Committees described their rationale for providing additional funds. The House Appropriations Committee noted that "These programs have been hit hard by rising food costs at the same time as demand for services is increasing because of the economic downturn and the growing elder population."[19] The Senate Appropriations Committee stated "The Committee notes that due to the current economic crisis, many local senior programs are closing meals sites and eliminating meal delivery routes. The additional funding provided will help offset these cutbacks, which put our most vulnerable seniors at risk of hunger, poor health and isolation."[20] According to AOA, ARRA funding has helped 20% of states eliminate waitlists for seniors requesting home-delivered meals. AOA also estimates that without ARRA funding, 8.1 million fewer meals would have been provided in FY2010.[21]

The FY2011 Budget requests $1.467 billion for Title III, an 8% increase over the FY2010 funding level. Most of this increase is due to a new Caregiver Initiative to help individuals with family caregiving responsibilities. The initiative stems from the work of the White House Task Force on Middle Class Families.[22] The Caregiver Initiative would provide a $48.0 million (13%) increase for Title III-B supportive services, such as adult day care, transportation to medical appointments and grocery stores, and personal care and chore services. AOA estimates that this additional funding would support 1 million additional hours of adult day care, 3 million additional rides, and 1.3 million additional hours of personal care services (such as assistance with eating, dressing, and bathing).[23] The Caregiver Initiative would also provide a $48.0 million (31%) increase for Title III-E family caregiver support services, such as respite care, training and counseling, and access assistance services (to help caregivers locate services from private and voluntary agencies). AOA estimates that this additional funding would provide services to nearly 200,000 additional caregivers.[24]

Under the FY2011 Budget, funding for Title III-C nutrition services would be $827.5 million, a 1% increase from the FY2010 level. AOA notes that the economic downturn has affected the budgets of states, tribes, local governments, philanthropies, and private donors that partner with AOA to provide meals. As a result, AOA projects that in FY2011, 14.7 million fewer meals will be provided than in FY2010, when 228.5 million meals would be provided.[25]

More background on Title III nutrition services is in CRS Report RS21202, *Older Americans Act: Title III Nutrition Services Program*, by Kirsten J. Colello.

## Title IV. Activities for Health, Independence, and Longevity

Title IV of the OAA authorizes the Assistant Secretary for Aging to award funds for training, research, and demonstration projects in the field of aging. In recent years, AOA has funded a number of national efforts that support the work of State and Area Agencies on Aging, including national resource centers that focus on legal assistance and the retirement needs of women, and technical assistance for National Minority Aging Organizations. Other recent projects have included the National Alzheimer's Call Center, funding for supportive services to older individuals in naturally occurring retirement communities,[26] and funding for ADRCs. Other activities have included outreach to help Medicare beneficiaries understand their benefits under the Medicare Modernization Act (MMA), conducted in cooperation with the Centers for Medicare and Medicaid Services.[27]

The FY2010 Omnibus Appropriations Act (P.L. 111-117) provides $19.0 million for Title IV, a 5% increase over the FY2009 level.

The FY2011 Budget requests $43.5 million for Title IV, a $24.5 million increase over the FY2010 level. This increase is due to the Budget's $30.5 million request for Health and Long-Term Care Programs under Title IV authority; previously Health and Long-Term Care Programs have been funded under Title II Aging Network Support Activities.[28] (See the discussion in the "Title II. Administration on Aging" section above). The FY2011 Budget also proposes that chronic disease self-management programs (CDSMPs), previously funded through Health and Long-Term Care Programs' Evidence-Based Disease Prevention component, instead be funded through a separate ARRA funding stream (the $32.5 million discussed in the "Title II. Administration on Aging" section above). Finally, the FY2011 Budget proposes to redirect funds currently being used in the Health and Long-Term Care Programs' Community Living Programs (CLP) component, and focus them instead "on new approaches that will complement the aging services network's role in health and long-term care reform, such as discharge planning."[29]

## Title V. Community Service Employment for Older Americans

Title V, also known as the Senior Community Service Employment Program (SCSEP), has as its purpose the promotion of useful part-time opportunities in community service activities for unemployed low-income[30] persons who are 55 years or older and who have poor employment prospects. For FY2010, the community service employment program represents 35% of the OAA's funds ($825.4 million out of $2.328 billion).

Enrollees work part-time in a variety of community service jobs, such as in day care centers, libraries, schools, and hospitals, as well as "green" assignments such as recycling and tree-planting programs.[31] The program operates on a program year (PY) basis from July 1 through June 30. In PY2009 (ending June 30, 2010), the DOL estimates that the program will provide for 66,179 job slots, serving about 99,269 participants, at a cost of $6,428 per participant.[32]

Enrollees are paid no less than the highest of the federal minimum wage, the state or local minimum wage, or the prevailing wage paid by the same employer for similar public occupations. In addition to wages, enrollees receive training, physical examinations, personal and job-related counseling, placement assistance into unsubsidized jobs, and transportation for employment purposes, under certain circumstances.

The 2006 Older Americans Act Amendments (P.L. 109-365) maintained the program focus on employing older people in community service jobs and reemphasized the community service aspects of the program. While the program's purpose is to move participants into unsubsidized employment, the amendments recognized that many older people who have special needs may need to remain in subsidized employment and that the program supplements the income for some workers who cannot find jobs in the private economy.[33]

In FY2009, Title V received $571.9 million from the Omnibus Appropriations Act (P.L. 111-8) and $120.0 million from ARRA (P.L. 111-5), totaling $691.9 million for Title V in FY2009. The ARRA conference report stated "The wages paid to these low-income seniors will provide a direct stimulus to the economies of local communities, which will also benefit from the community service work performed by participants."[34]

ARRA made the additional Title V funds available from the date of enactment through June 30, 2010. ARRA required the funds to be allotted within 30 days of enactment to current grantees in proportion to their program year 2008 allotment.[35] Furthermore, the Secretary of Labor would be allowed to recapture any unexpended funds for the program year, and reobligate them within the next two program years, in accordance with section 517(c) of the Older Americans Act.

The FY2010 funding level of $825.4 million is $253.5 million (44%) higher than the level provided in the FY2009 Omnibus Appropriations Act, and $133.5 million (19%) higher than the total FY2009 level (including both the Omnibus and ARRA).[36] The conference report accompanying the FY2010 Consolidated Appropriations Act states that "additional resources provided in the Recovery Act are insufficient to meet the needs of low-income older workers adversely impacted by the recession. Many CSEOA [Community Service Employment for Older Americans] grantees are maintaining waiting lists for available community service jobs but are unable to fill those jobs due to funding limitations."[37]

The FY2010 Consolidated Appropriations Act made $225.0 million available upon enactment, to remain available through December 31, 2011. The conference report stated "In determining those current grantees that can effectively use funds made available immediately in this Act, the Secretary should take into account demonstrated need, financial management, and sustained and satisfactory performance."[38] DOL explains that this funding "was intended as a one-time provision related to current economic conditions. The additional funding was provided as a short-term program expansion to support temporary job opportunities for low-income elderly individuals while the nation recovers from the economic downturn."[39]

The FY2011 Budget requests $600.4 million for Title V, or $225.0 million (27%) less than the FY2010 funding level. The DOL estimates that the requested FY2011 funding level would serve 92,024 participants in 61,893 job slots.[40]

## Title VI. Grants for Services for Native Americans

Title VI authorizes funds for supportive and nutrition services to older Native Americans. Funds are awarded directly by AOA to Indian tribal organizations, Native Alaskan organizations, and non-profit groups representing Native Hawaiians. To be eligible for funding, a tribal organization must represent at least 50 Native American elders age 60 or older. In FY2009, grants were awarded to 244 tribal organizations representing approximately 400 Indian tribes and two organizations serving Native Hawaiian elders.[41] The program provides services such as transportation, home-delivered and congregate nutrition services, information and referral, and a wide range of home care services.

The 2000 amendments (P.L. 106-501) added a new part to Title VI authorizing caregiver support services to Native American elders. Respite, caregiver training, information and outreach, counseling, and support groups are among the services provided.

The FY2010 Consolidated Appropriations Act (P.L. 111-117) provides $34.1 million for Title VI, a 1% increase over the funding level in the FY2009 Omnibus Appropriations Act (P.L. 111-8), and a 7% decrease from the total FY2009 funding level (counting both the Omnibus and ARRA). In FY2009, ARRA had provided an additional $3 million for nutrition services for Native Americans under Title VI.[42]

The FY2011 Budget requests $38.1 million for Title VI, a $4.0 million (12%) increase over the FY2010 level. The increase would be due to the Caregiver Initiative (discussed in the "Title III. Grants for State and Community Programs on Aging" section above), which would provide a $2.0

million increase for Title VI supportive services, and a $2.0 million increase for Title VI-C caregiver support services.

## Title VII. Vulnerable Elder Rights Protection Activities

Title VII authorizes the long-term care ombudsman program as well as elder abuse, neglect, and exploitation prevention programs. Most Title VII funding is directed at the long-term care ombudsman program. Of its $21.9 million funding in FY2010, more than three-quarters ($16.8 million) is for ombudsman activities. The purpose of the program is to investigate and resolve complaints of residents of nursing facilities, board and care facilities, and other adult care homes. In FY2008, ombudsmen handled nearly 272,000 complaints, conducted investigations on almost 185,000 cases, and provided more than 455,000 consultations to individuals and long-term care facilities.[43] More background on the ombudsman program can be found in CRS Report RS21297, *Older Americans Act: Long-Term Care Ombudsman Program*, by Kirsten J. Colello.

The FY2010 Consolidated Appropriations Act (P.L. 111-117) provides $21.9 million for Title VII, a 2% increase over the FY2009 level. The FY2011 Budget requests $23.3 million for Title VII, a 6% increase over the FY2010 level.[44]

## OTHER PROGRAMS ADMINISTERED BY AOA

The AOA also administers the Alzheimer's Disease Supportive Services Program and the Lifespan Respite Care Program. Both programs, described in greater detail below, are authorized under the PHSA and not the OAA. In addition to these two programs, AOA has received funding to organize and convene the White House Conference on Aging (WHCOA), which, once a decade, makes aging policy recommendations to the President and Congress. The last conference occurred in 2005 and was authorized under the OAA amendments of 2000 (P.L. 106-501).

## Alzheimer's Disease Supportive Services Program

The Alzheimer's Disease Supportive Services Program (ADSSP) Program [formerly known as the Alzheimer's Disease Demonstration Grants to States (ADDGS) Program] aims to improve and expand home and community-based care and other supportive services for persons with Alzheimer's Disease and Related Disorders (ADRD) and their caregivers. Between 2007 and 2009, AOA awarded 47 ADSSP cooperative agreements to states to implement such projects across the United States.[45] Although current authorization under Section 398B of the PHSA has expired, Congress continues to appropriate funding.[46] The FY2010 Consolidated Appropriations Act (P.L. 111-117) funds ADDGS at $11.5 million, the same as the FY2009 level. The FY2011 Budget proposes to maintain funding at $11.5 million.

## Lifespan Respite Care

The Lifespan Respite Care Program awards matching grants to eligible state agencies to (1) develop or enhance lifespan respite care activities at the state and local levels; (2) improve the statewide dissemination and coordination of respite care; and (3) provide, supplement, or improve access and quality of respite care services to family caregivers caring for children and adults. The law defines "respite care" to mean planned or emergency care provided to a child or adult of any age with a special need in order to give temporary relief to the family caregiver. The program was enacted under the Lifespan Respite Care Act of 2006 (P.L. 109-442), which amended the PHSA to create a new Title XXIX authorizing appropriations totaling $289 million for FY2007 through FY2011; however, Congress first appropriated funding for Lifespan Respite Care Program activities in FY2009. In September 2009, AOA awarded grants to 12 states to implement the program.[47] The FY2010 Consolidated Appropriation Act (P.L. 111-117) provides $2.5 million for Lifespan Respite Care, the same as the FY2009 level. As part of the Caregiver Initiative, the FY2011 Budget proposes to double funding to $5.0 million.[48]

# Appendix A. Older Americans Act and Other AOA Programs: FY2003-FY2010 Funding

Table A-1 shows appropriations history for the act's programs for FY2003-FY2010. In addition, the appropriations histories for other programs administered by AOA are also provided.

## Table A-1. Funding for the Older Americans Act, Alzheimer's Supportive Services, White House Conference on Aging, and Lifespan Respite Care, FY2003-FY2010 ($ in millions)

| OAA Programs, Alzheimer's Supportive Services, White House Conference on Aging, and Lifespan Respite Care | FY2003 | FY2004 | FY2005[a] | FY2006[b] | FY2007[c] | FY2008[d] | FY2009 Omnibus (P.L. 111-8) | FY2009 American Recovery and Reinvestment Act (P.L. 111-5) | FY2010 |
|---|---|---|---|---|---|---|---|---|---|
| Title II: Administration on Aging | $20.233 | $30.618 | $31.567 | $30.812 | $31.518 | $49.653 | $60.390 | 0 | $64.262 |
| Program administration | 17.869 | 17.324 | 18.301 | 17.688 | 18.385 | 18.064 | 18.696 | 0 | 19.979 |
| Aging network support activities | 2.364[e] | 13.294[f] | 13.266 | 13.124 | 13.133 | 31.589[g] | 41.694[h] | 0 | 44.283[i] |
| Title III: Grants for State and Community Programs on Aging | 1,240.891 | 1,243.059 | 1,250.192 | 1,242.378 | 1,263.232 | 1,283.816 | 1,346.337 | 97.000[j] | 1,363.068 |

## Table A-1. (Continued)

| OAA Programs, Alzheimer's Supportive Services, White House Conference on Aging, and Lifespan Respite Care | FY2003 | FY2004 | FY2005[a] | FY2006[b] | FY2007[c] | FY2008[d] | FY2009 Omnibus (P.L. 111-8) | FY2009 American Recovery and Reinvestment Act (P.L. 111-5) | FY2010 |
|---|---|---|---|---|---|---|---|---|---|
| Supportive services and centers | 355.673 | 353.889 | 354.136 | 350.354 | 350.595 | 351.348 | 361.348 | 0 | 368.348 |
| Family caregivers[k] | 149.025 | 152.738 | 155.744 | 156.060 | 156.167 | 153.439 | 154.220 | 0 | 154.220 |
| Disease prevention/health promotion | 21.919 | 21.970 | 21.616 | 21.385 | 21.400 | 21.026 | 21.026 | 0 | 21.026 |
| Nutrition services | 714.274 | 714.462 | 718.696 | 714.579 | 735.070 | 758.003 | 809.743 | 97.0001 | 819.474 |
| Congregate meals | (384.592) | (386.353) | (387.274) | (385.054) | (398.919)[n] | (410.716) | (434.269) | (65.000)[m] | (440.783) |
| Home-delivered meals | (180.985) | (179.917) | (182.826) | (181.781) | (188.305)[n] | (193.858) | (214.459) | (32.000)[o] | (217.676) |
| Nutrition services incentive grants | (148.697)[p] | (148.192) | (148.596) | (147.744) | (147.846) | (153.429) | (161.015) | 0 | (161.015) |
| Title IV: Activities for Health, Independence, and Longevity[q] | 40.258 | 33.509[r] | 43.286 | 24.578 | 24.058 | 14.655 | 18.172 | 0 | 19.023 |
| Title V: Community Service Employment for Older Americans | 442.306 | 438.650 | 436.678 | 432.311 | 483.611[n] | 521.625 | 571.925 | 120.000[s] | 825.425 |
| Title VI: Grants to Native Americans | 33.704 | 32.771 | 32.702 | 32.353 | 32.375 | 33.214 | 33.597 | 3.000[t] | 34.097 |

Table A-1. (Continued)

| OAA Programs, Alzheimer's Supportive Services, White House Conference on Aging, and Lifespan Respite Care | FY2003 | FY2004 | FY2005[a] | FY2006[b] | FY2007[c] | FY2008[d] | FY2009 Omnibus (P.L. 111-8) | FY2009 American Recovery and Reinvestment Act (P.L. 111-5) | FY2010 |
|---|---|---|---|---|---|---|---|---|---|
| Supportive and nutrition services | 27.495 | 26.453 | 26.398 | 26.116 | 26.134 | 26.898 | 27.208 | 3.000[u] | 27.708 |
| Native American caregiversv | 6.209 | 6.318 | 6.304 | 6.237 | 6.241 | 6.316 | 6.389 | 0 | 6.389 |
| Title VII: Vulnerable Elder Rights Protection Activities | 18.559 | 19.444 | 19.288 | 20.142 | 20.156 | 20.633 | 21.383 | 0 | 21.883 |
| Long-term care ombudsman program | n/a[w] | 14.276 | 14.162 | 15.000 | 15.010 | 15.577[x] | 16.327 | 0 | 16.827 |
| Elder abuse prevention | n/a[w] | 5.168 | 5.126 | 5.142 | 5.146 | 5.056 | 5.056 | 0 | 5.056 |
| Legal assistance | 0 | 0 | 0 | 0 | 0 | 0 | 0 | 0 | 0 |
| Native Americans elder rights program | 0 | 0 | 0 | 0 | 0 | 0 | 0 | 0 | 0 |
| Total Older Americans Act Programs | $1,771.057 | $1,798.051 | $1,813.713 | $1,782.574 | $1,854.950 | $1,923.596 | $2,051.804 | $220.000[y] | $2,327.758 |
| Alzheimer's Disease Supportive Services Program[z] | $13.412 | $11.883 | $11.786 | $11.660 | $11.668 | $11.464 | $11.464 | 0 | $11.464 |

Table A-1. (Continued)

| OAA Programs, Alzheimer's Supportive Services, White House Conference on Aging, and Lifespan Respite Care | FY2003 | FY2004 | FY2005[a] | FY2006[b] | FY2007[c] | FY2008[d] | FY2009 Omnibus (P.L. 111-8) | FY2009 American Recovery and Reinvestment Act (P.L. 111-5) | FY2010 |
|---|---|---|---|---|---|---|---|---|---|
| White House Conference on Aging | 0 | $2.814[aa] | $4.520[aa] | 0[aa] | 0 | 0 | 0 | 0 | 0 |
| Lifespan Respite Care | | | | | | | $2.500[bb] | 0 | $2.500[bb] |

Source: FY2003-FY2006: Appropriations legislation and committee reports, various years. FY2007-FY2008: Consolidated Appropriations Act, 2008, Committee Print of the Committee on Appropriations, U.S. House of Representatives, on H.R. 2764 / P.L. 110-161, January, 2008, pp. 1776, 1809-1810, http://www.gpoaccess.gov/congress/ house/appropriations/08conappro.html. FY2009: "Explanatory Statement Submitted by Mr. Obey, Chairman of the House Committee on Appropriations, Regarding H.R. 1105, Omnibus Appropriations Act, 2009," *Congressional Record*, February 23, 2009, pp. H2372, H2385; H.Rept. 111-16, *Conference Report to Accompany H.R. 1*, pp. 449, 455. FY20 10: H.Rept. 111-366, *Conference Report to Accompany H.R. 3288*, pp. 989, 1298-1299; Administration on Aging, *FY2010 Appropriation*, http://www.aoa.gov/AoARoot/ About/Budget/docs/Appropriation_FY_20 10.pdf

a. FY2005 amounts reflect the 0.80% across-the-board reduction required by P.L. 108-447, Division J, Section 122. The Administration was given discretion on how to distribute the reduction among individual accounts and line items.

b. FY2006 amounts reflect two rescissions: (1) There was a 1% across-the-board reduction required by P.L. 109-148, Division B, Title III, Chapter 8, Section 3801. (2) On June 14, 2006, the HHS Secretary notified the Appropriations Committees that he would transfer funds among HHS programs to finance activities related to the Medicare drug benefit call center. This transfer was a 0.069% across-the-board reduction and it reduced Administration on Aging funds by $0.9 million. It was authorized by Section 208 of P.L. 109-149.

c. For FY2007, P.L. 110-5 specified dollar amounts for some, but not all, programs. Agencies had some flexibility to determine program amounts based on FY2006 appropriations.

d. P.L. 110-161, the FY2008 Consolidated Appropriations Act, applied an across-the-board reduction of 1.747% to figures in the bill text and Explanatory Statement narrative (Division G, Title V, §528).

e. Includes approximately $1.2 million for the Eldercare Locator, and $1.2 million for Pension Counseling and Information Program. These programs were authorized by the Older Americans Act Amendments of 2000 (P.L. 106-501, §205).

f. Starting in FY2004, Aging network support activities include funds for activities previously funded under Title IV: Senior Medicare Patrols, National Long-Term Care Ombudsman Resource Center, and National Center on Elder Abuse. Also includes funds for the Eldercare Locator, and Pension Counseling and Information Program.

g. The Choices for Independence Initiative included newly authorized provisions of the Older Americans Act Amendments of 2006 (P.L. 109-365) related to "aging and disability resource centers (ADRCs), evidence-based prevention programs, and consumer-directed services targeted at individuals who are at high risk of nursing home placement and spend-down to Medicaid" (H.Rept. 110-231, p. 207). The Bush Administration's FY2008 budget requested Choices for Independence funds under Title IV, while the FY2008 Consolidated Appropriations Act (P.L. 110-161) provided the funds under Aging Network support activities under Title II. The President's FY2008 budget request would have provided $28.0 million for Choices for Independence. P.L. 110-161 provided $16.2 million for Choices for Independence (after a 1.747% across-the-board reduction). Choices for Independence was subsequently renamed "Health and Long-Term Care Programs" in the Obama Administration's FY2010 budget request.

h. Includes $28.0 million for Choices for Independence. The Bush Administration's FY2009 budget request would have funded Choices for Independence at $28.0 million under Title IV, which authorizes funds for training, research, and demonstration projects.

i. Includes $30.589 million for Health and Long-Term Care Programs (formerly known as Choices for Independence). This is the same as the President's FY2010 budget request.

j. Total FY2009 funding for Title III was $1,443.337 million. This includes $1,346.337 million from the FY2009 Omnibus Appropriations Act (P.L. 111-8) and $97.000 million from the American Recovery and Reinvestment Act (P.L. 111-5).

k. Authorized by the Older Americans Act Amendments of 2000 (P.L. 106-501, §316). Funding for Native American family caregiving is shown in Title VI.

l. Total FY2009 funding for Title III-C Nutrition Services was $906.743 million. This Includes $809.743 million from the FY2009 Omnibus Appropriations Act (P.L. 111-8) and $97.000 million from the American Recovery and Reinvestment Act (P.L. 111-5).

m. Total FY2009 funding for congregate meals was $499.269 million. This includes $434.269 million from the FY2009 Omnibus Appropriations Act (P.L. 111-8) and $65.000 million from the American Recovery and Reinvestment Act (P.L. 111-5).
n. Funding level was specified in P.L. 110-5, Revised Continuing Appropriations Resolution, 2007.
o. Total FY2009 funding for home-delivered meals was $246.459 million. This includes $214.459 million from the FY2009 Omnibus Appropriations Act (P.L. 111-8) and $32.000 million from the American Recovery and Reinvestment Act (P.L. 111-5).
p. Congress transferred the program, previously funded by the U.S. Department of Agriculture, to the Administration on Aging in FY2003. P.L. 110-19 repealed certain provisions regarding state agency and tribal grantee commodity purchases, as added by the Older Americans Act Amendments of 2006 (P.L. 109-365), and restored former commodity purchase provisions, with revisions.
q. The Older Americans Act Amendments of 2006 (P.L. 109-365) renamed Title IV, formerly titled "Training, Research, and Discretionary Projects and Programs." Activities under Title IV are also sometimes referred to as "Program Innovations."
r. See tablenote f. Funds shown are reduced from FY2003 level due to transfer of some funds to Title II.
s. Total FY2009 funding for Title V was $69 1.925 million. This includes $57 1.925 million from the FY2009 Omnibus Appropriations Act (P.L. 111-8) and $ 120.000 million from the American Recovery and Reinvestment Act (P.L. 111-5).
t. Total FY2009 funding for Title VI was $36.597 million. This includes $33.597 million from the FY2009 Omnibus Appropriations Act (P.L. 111-8) and $3.000 million from the American Recovery and Reinvestment Act (P.L. 111-5).
u. Total FY2009 funding for supportive and nutrition services to Native Americans was $30.208 million. This includes $27.208 million from the FY2009 Omnibus Appropriations Act (P.L. 111-8) and $3.000 million from the American Recovery and Reinvestment Act (P.L. 111-5).
v. Authorized by the Older Americans Act Amendments of 2000 (P.L. 106-501, §604).
w. Separate amounts not specified.
x. Separate amounts not specified in FY2008 Consolidated Appropriations Act tables. These figures were calculated by CRS by applying the 1.747% across-the-board reduction to figures in the Explanatory Statement narrative in the *Congressional Record*, December 17, 2007, p. H 16242.
y. Total FY2009 funding for Older Americans Act programs was $2,271 .804 million. This includes $2,051 .804 million from the FY2009 Omnibus Appropriations Act (P.L. 111-8) and $220.000 million from the American Recovery and Reinvestment Act (P.L. 111-5).

z. Formerly known as Alzheimer's Disease Demonstration Grants to the States. The FY1999 Omnibus Consolidated Appropriations Act (P.L. 105-277) transferred the administration of the program from the Health Resources and Services Administration to the Administration on Aging. The program was authorized under Sections 398 to 398B of the Public Health Service Act (42 U.S.C. §§ 280c-3 to 280c-5). Authorization of appropriations expired in 2002.

aa. P.L. 106-501 required the President to convene the conference no later than December 31, 2005. It was held December 11-14, 2005. See http://www.whcoa.gov. FY2006 obligations for the White House Conference on Aging were funded by carryover balances of prior-year appropriations.

bb. The Lifespan Respite Care program is authorized by Title XXIX of the Public Health Service Act (42 U.S.C. §§ 300ii to 300ii-4). It is administered by the Administration on Aging. The Lifespan Respite Care program received its first funding in FY2009.

# APPENDIX B. OLDER AMERICANS ACT AND OTHER AOA PROGRAMS: FY2010 FUNDING AND FY2011 BUDGET REQUEST

Table B-1. FY2010 Funding and FY2011 Budget Request for the Older Americans Act, Alzheimer's Supportive Services, and Lifespan Respite Care ($ in millions)

|  | FY2010 | FY2011 Request | Proposed change |
|---|---|---|---|
| **Title II: Administration on Aging** | $64.262 | $36.202 | -44% |
| Program administration | 19.979 | 22.508 | +13% |
| Aging network support activities | 44.283 | 13.694 | -69% |
| Health and Long-Term Care Programs | (30.589) | a | -100% [a] |
| Aging network support activities, excluding Health and Long-Term Care Programs | (13.694) | (13.694) | 0 |
| **Title III: Grants for State and Community Programs on Aging** | 1,363.068 | 1,467.146 | +8% |
| Supportive services and centers | 368.348 | 416.348b | +13% [b] |
| Family caregivers[c] | 154.220 | 202.220b | +31% [b] |
| Disease prevention/health promotion | 21.026 | 21.026 | 0 |
| Nutrition services | 819.474 | 827.552 | +1% |
| Congregate meals | (440.783) | (445.644) | +1% |
| Home-delivered meals | (217.676) | (220.893) | +1% |
| Nutrition services incentive grants | (161.015) | (161.015) | 0 |
| **Title IV: Activities for Health, Independence, and Longevity** | 19.023 | 43.534 | +129% |
| Program Innovations | 19.023 | 13.049 | -31% |
| Health and Long-Term Care Programs | a | 30.485 | a |
| **Title V: Community Service Employment for Older Americans** | 825.425 | 600.425 | -27% |
| **Title VI: Grants to Native Americans** | 34.097 | 38.097 | +12% [b] |
| Supportive and nutrition services | 27.708 | 29.708[b] | +7% [b] |
| Native American caregivers | 6.389 | 8.389[b] | +31% [b] |
| **Title VII: Vulnerable Elder Rights Protection Activities** | 21.883 | 23.290 | +6% |
| Long-term care ombudsman program | 16.827 | 17.783 | +6% |
| Elder abuse prevention | 5.056 | 5.507 | +9% |
| Legal assistance | 0 | 0 | 0 |
| Native Americans elder rights program | 0 | 0 | 0 |
| **Total Older Americans Act Programs** | $2,327.758 | $2,208.694 | -5% |
| Alzheimer's Disease Supportive Services Program[d] | $11.464 | $11.464 | 0 |
| Lifespan Respite Care[e] | $2.500 | $5.000[b] | +100% [b] |

Source: FY2010: H.Rept. 111-366, *Conference Report to Accompany H.R. 3288*, pp. 989, 1298-1299; Administration on Aging, *FY20 10 Appropriation*, http://www.aoa.gov/AoARoot/About/Budget/docs/ Appropriation_FY_20 10.pdf. FY20 11: Department of Labor, *FY2011 Congressional Budget Justification, Employment and Training Administration, Community Service Employment for Older Americans*, pp. CSEOA- 12, http://www.dol.gov/ dol/budget/20 11 /PDF/CBJ-20 11-V 1 -06.pdf; Administration on Aging, *Fiscal Year 2011 Justification of Estimates for Appropriations Committees*, p. 15, http://www.aoa.gov/AoAroot/ About/Budget/ DOCS/AoA_CJ_FY_2011.pdf

a. The FY2011 Budget requests funding for Health and Long-Term Care Programs under Title IV authority. Previously it has been funded as part of Aging network support activities under Title II.
b. The FY2011 Budget proposes a $102.5 million Caregiver Initiative that would increase funding for services to help family caregivers. The Caregiver Initiative proposes a $48.0 million increase for supportive services and a $48.0 million increase for family caregiver support services, both under Title III. The Caregiver Initiative also proposes a $2.0 million increase for Native American supportive services and a $2.0 million increase for Native American caregiver support services, both under Title VI. Finally, the Caregiver Initiative proposes a $2.5 million increase for Lifespan Respite Care (authorized by the Public Health Service Act).
c. Funding for Native American family caregiving is shown in Title VI.
d. Formerly known as Alzheimer's Disease Demonstration Grants to the States. The program was authorized under Sections 398 to 398B of the Public Health Service Act (42 U.S.C. §§ 280c-3 to 280c-5). Authorization of appropriations expired in 2002.
e. The Lifespan Respite Care program is authorized by Title XXIX of the Public Health Service Act (42 U.S.C. §§ 300ii to 300ii-4). It is administered by the Administration on Aging.

# APPENDIX C. OLDER AMERICANS ACT: AUTHORIZATION OF APPROPRIATIONS

Table C-1 shows the authorization of appropriations for each title of the act as stipulated by the 2006 Older Americans Act Amendments (P.L. 109-365).

## Table C-1. Authorization of Appropriations for Older Americans Act Programs in P.L. 109-365

| Older Americans Act Programs | Authorization of Appropriations |
|---|---|
| **Title II, Administration on Aging** | |
| Administration on Aging | FY2007-FY2011, such sums as may be necessary. |
| Eldercare Locator | FY2007-FY2011, such sums as may be necessary. |
| Pension counseling and information program | FY2007-FY2011, such sums as may be necessary. |
| **Title III, State and Community Programs on Aging** | |
| Supportive services and centers | FY2007-FY2011, such sums as may be necessary. |
| Congregate nutrition services | FY2007-FY2011, such sums as may be necessary. |
| Home-delivered nutrition services | FY2007-FY2011, such sums as may be necessary. |
| Disease prevention and health promotion | FY2007-FY2011, such sums as may be necessary. |
| Family caregiver support | FY2007, $160.0 million; FY2008, $165.5 million; FY2009, $173.0 million; FY2010, $180.0 million; FY2011, $187.0 million. |
| Nutrition services incentive program (formerly the USDA commodity or cash-in-lieu of commodities program) | FY2007-FY2011, such sums as may be necessary. |
| **Title IV, Activities for Health, Independence, and Longevity** | |
| FY2007-FY2011, such sums as may be necessary. | |
| **Title V, Community Service Senior Opportunities Act** | |
| FY2007-FY2011, such sums as may be necessary. | |
| **Title VI, Grants for Native Americans** | |
| Indian and Native Hawaiian programs | FY2007-FY2011, such sums as may be necessary. |
| Native American caregiver support program | FY2007, $6.5 million; FY2008, $6.8 million; FY2009, $7.2 million; FY2010, $7.5 million; FY2011, $7.9 million. |
| **Title VII, Vulnerable Elder Rights Protection Activities** | |
| **Subtitle A—State Programs** | |
| Long-term care ombudsman program | FY2007-FY2011, such sums as may be necessary. |
| Elder abuse, neglect, and exploitation prevention program | FY2007-FY2011, such sums as may be necessary. |
| Legal assistance development program | FY2007-FY2011, such sums as may be necessary. |
| **Subtitle B—Native American Organization and Elder Justice Provisions** | |
| Native American elder rights program | FY2007-FY2011, such sums as may be necessary. |
| Grants for state elder justice systems | No authorization specified. |

# APPENDIX D. OLDER AMERICANS ACT: HISTORICAL DEVELOPMENT

Congress created the Older Americans Act (OAA) in 1965 in response to concern by policymakers about a lack of community social services for older persons. The original legislation established authority for grants to states for community planning and social services, research and development projects, and personnel training in the field of aging. The law also established the Administration on Aging (AOA) within the then-Department of Health, Education, and Welfare (DHEW) to administer the newly created grant programs and to serve as the federal focal point on matters concerning older persons.

Although older persons may receive services under many other federal programs, today the act is considered to be the major vehicle for the organization and delivery of social and nutrition services to this group. It authorizes a wide array of service programs through a nationwide network of 57 state agencies on aging and 655 area agencies on aging, supports the sole federal job creation program benefitting low-income older workers, and funds training, research, and demonstration activities in the field of aging.

Prior to the creation of the act in 1965, older persons were eligible for limited social services through some federal programs. However, with the recognition that older persons were becoming an increasing proportion of the population and that their needs were not being formally addressed through existing programs, many groups began advocating on their behalf. Their actions led President Truman to initiate the first National Conference on Aging in 1950. Conferees called for government and voluntary agencies to accept greater responsibility for the problems and welfare of older persons. Further interest in the field of aging led President Eisenhower to create the Federal Council on Aging in 1956 to coordinate the activities of the various units of the federal government related to aging.

The beginning of a major thrust toward legislation along the lines of the later-enacted OAA was made at the 1961 White House Conference on Aging (WHCOA). The conferees called for a federal coordinating agency in the field of aging to be set up on a statutory basis, with adequate funding for coordinating federal efforts in aging, as well as a federal program of grants for community services specifically for the elderly.[49]

In response to the WHCOA recommendations, Representative John Fogarty of Rhode Island and Senator Pat McNamara of Michigan introduced legislation in 1962 to establish an independent U.S. Committee on Aging to cut across the responsibilities of many departments and agencies, and create a program of grants for social services, research, and training that would benefit older persons. Because there were objections by the Administration to the creation of an independent federal agency on aging, the legislation was not enacted. Legislation introduced the following year by Representative Fogarty and Senator McNamara modified the 1962 proposal by creating within DHEW the AOA, which was to be under the direction of a Commissioner for Aging, appointed by the President with the approval of the Senate. However, the 1963 proposal was not enacted.

The OAA as introduced in 1965 basically paralleled the 1963 proposal. Sponsors emphasized how it would provide resources necessary for public and private social service providers to meet the social service needs of the elderly. The act received wide bipartisan support and was signed into law by President Johnson on July 14, 1965. In addition to creating AOA, the act authorized grants to states for community planning and services programs, as well as for research, demonstration, and training projects in the field of aging. In his remarks upon signing the bill, the President indicated that the legislation would provide "an orderly, intelligent, and constructive program to help us meet the new dimensions of responsibilities which lie ahead in the remaining years of this century. Under this program every state and every community can now move toward a coordinated program of services and opportunities for our older citizens."[50]

## Major Amendments to the Older Americans Act

Since the original legislation was enacted in 1965, the OAA (P.L. 89-73) has been amended numerous times. The following provides a summary of major amendments to the OAA over the past four decades.

### *1960s*

The first amendments to the act in 1967 extended authorization for the state grant program and for research, demonstration, and training programs created in 1965. In 1969, Congress added authority for a program of area-wide model projects to test new and varied approaches to meet the social service needs of the elderly. The 1969 amendments also authorized the foster grandparent and retired senior volunteer programs to provide part-time volunteer opportunities for the elderly. (Authority for volunteer programs was subsequently repealed and these programs were reauthorized under the Domestic Volunteer Service Act of 1973.)

## *1970s*

Major amendments to the act occurred in 1972 with the creation of the national nutrition program for the elderly. The 1973 amendments represented a major shift in federal law with the establishment of substate area agencies on aging. For the first time, Congress authorized the creation of local agencies whose purpose is to plan and coordinate services for older persons and to act as advocates for programs on their behalf. These amendments also created legislative authority for the community service employment program for older Americans which had previously operated as a demonstration initiative under the Economic Opportunity Act. In 1974, Congress passed legislation to extend the national nutrition program for the elderly. The 1975 amendments extended the OAA through 1978, specifying certain services to receive funding priority under the state and area agency on aging program. In 1977, Congress made changes to the OAA nutrition program primarily related to surplus commodities.

The 1978 amendments represented a major structural change to the act when the separate grant programs for social services, nutrition services, and multipurpose senior center facilities were consolidated into one program under the authority of state and area agencies on aging. The intent of these amendments was to improve coordination among the various service programs under the act. Among other changes were requirements for establishing state long-term care ombudsman programs and a new Title VI authorizing grants to Indian tribal organizations for social and nutrition services to older Indians.

## *1980s*

The 1981 amendments made modifications to give state and area agencies on aging (AAAs) more flexibility in the administration of their service programs. These amendments also emphasized the transition of participants to private sector employment under the community service employment program. In 1984, Congress enacted a number of provisions, including adding responsibilities for AOA; adding provisions designed to target services on low-income minority older persons; giving more flexibility to states regarding service funds allocations; and giving priority to the needs of Alzheimer's victims and their families. The 1986 amendments increased authorized appropriations to provide a higher per meal reimbursement rate and directed the Secretary of Agriculture and HHS to inform state, AAA's, and meal providers of their eligibility to participate in the National Commodity Processing Program.

The 1987 amendments expanded certain service components of the state and area agency program to address the special needs of certain populations. Congress authorized six additional distinct authorizations of appropriations for services: in-home services for the frail elderly; longterm care ombudsman services; assistance for special needs; health education and promotion services; services to prevent abuse, neglect and exploitation of older individuals; and outreach activities for persons who may be eligible for benefits under the supplemental security income (S SI), Medicaid and food stamp programs. Among other changes were provisions designed to give special attention to the needs of older Native Americans and persons with disabilities, emphasize targeting of services to those most in need, elevate the status of AOA within the Department of Health and Human Services (HHS), and liberalize eligibility of community service employment participants for other federal programs.

## *1990s*

The 1992 amendments restructured some of the act's programs. A new Title VII, Vulnerable Elder Rights Protection Activities, was created to consolidate and expand certain programs that focus on protection of the rights of older persons. Title VII incorporated separate authorizations of appropriations for the long-term care ombudsman program; program for the prevention of elder abuse, neglect, and exploitation; elder rights and legal assistance development program; and outreach, counseling, and assistance for insurance and public benefit programs. In addition, provisions were included to strengthen requirements related to targeting of Title III services on special population groups. Other amendments authorized programs for assistance to caregivers of the frail elderly; clarified the role of Title III agencies in working with the for-profit sector; and required improvements in AOA data collection.

In 1993, Congress amended the OAA to establish an Assistant Secretary for Aging (formerly the Commissioner on Aging) within HHS, extended the time frame for convening the White House Conference on Aging, and made technical amendments to the act and several other acts.

## *2000s*

The 2000 amendments were enacted after six years of congressional debate on reauthorization. P.L. 106-501 extended the act's programs through FY2005. These amendments authorized the National Family Caregiver

Support Program under Title III; required the Secretary of the Department of Labor (DOL) to establish performance measures for the senior community service employment program; allowed states to impose cost-sharing for certain Title III services older persons receive while retaining authority for voluntary contributions by older persons toward the costs of services; and consolidated a number of previously separately authorized programs. In addition, the amendments required the President to convene a WHCOA by December 31, 2005.

In 2003, Congress amended the OAA to revise provisions for the Nutrition Services Incentives Program whereby maintaining access to commodities within the Department of Agriculture, but transferring authority for such program from the Department of Agriculture to AOA.

The 2006 amendments extended the act's programs through FY2011. Among other things, the law authorized the Assistant Secretary on Aging to designate an individual within AOA to be responsible for prevention of elder abuse, neglect and exploitation and to coordinate federal elder justice activities. It revised the formula for the allocation of Title III funds and revised the Title V community service employment program to place more emphasis on training of older individuals, while maintaining emphasis on employing them in community service activities. The law also required the Secretary of Labor to conduct a national competition for Title V funds every four years. The 2006 amendments also required states to conduct increased planning efforts related to the growing number of older people in coming decades; and focused attention on the needs of older people with limited English proficiency and those at risk of institutional placement. The law added authority for the Assistant Secretary on Aging to conduct several new demonstration programs under Title IV. Among these are demonstration projects for model projects to assist older people to age in place, including in Naturally Occurring Retirement Communities (NORCs).

## ACKNOWLEDGMENTS

Parts of this report were originally authored by Carol O'Shaughnessy. The graphics were created by Pat McClaughry.

## End Notes

[1] The Older Americans Act Amendments of 2006 (P.L. 109-3 65) reauthorized all OAA programs through FY20 11. For further information, see CRS Report RL3 1336, *The Older Americans Act: Programs, Funding, and 2006 Reauthorization (P.L. 109-365)*, by Carol O'Shaughnessy and Angela Napili. An unofficial compilation of the OAA, as amended, is at the Administration on Aging (AOA) website, at http://www.aoa.gov/AoARoot/AoA_Programs/OAA.

[2] The National Eldercare Locator can be reached through http://www.eldercare.gov or 1-800-677-1116.

[3] Funding for the National Center for Senior Benefits Outreach and Enrollment began in FY2008. More information is at http://www.aoa.gov/AoARoot/ AoA_Programs/HCLTC/Senior_Benefits/index.aspx and http://www.centerforbenefits.org/.

[4] HHS, AOA, *Fiscal Year 2010 Justification of Estimates for Appropriations Committees*, pp. 70-71, http://www.aoa.gov/AoARoot/Program_Results/docs/2010/FY2010AoACongressionalJustificationFinal.PDF.

[5] HHS, AOA, *Fiscal Year 2011 Justification of Estimates for Appropriations Committees*, p. 89, http://www.aoa.gov/ AoAroot/About/Budget/DOCS/AoA_CJ_FY_201 1.pdf.

[6] AOA, *Aging and Disability Resource Center Fact Sheet*, http://www.aoa.gov/AoARoot/Press_Room/ Products _Materials/fact/pdf/ADRC.pdf. A directory of ADRCs is at the Aging and Disability Resource Center Technical Assistance Exchange website at http://www.adrc-tae.org/tiki-index.php?page=ADRCLocator.

[7] HHS, AOA, *Fiscal Year 2011 Justification of Estimates for Appropriations Committees*, p. 91.

[8] HHS, AOA, *Fiscal Year 2010 Justification of Estimates for Appropriations Committees*, pp. 69-71.

[9] HHS, AOA, *Fiscal Year 2011 Justification of Estimates for Appropriations Committees*, p. 89. For more information on Cash and Counseling see http://www.cashandcounseling.org.

[10] The $32.5 million for CDSMP activities would come from the $650 million that ARRA provided to HHS for evidence-based prevention and wellness programs. The ARRA provisions are described in CRS Report R40 181, *Selected Health Funding in the American Recovery and Reinvestment Act of 2009*, coordinated by C. Stephen Redhead.

[11] For more background, see AOA, *American Recovery and Reinvestment Act: Communities Putting Prevention to Work: Chronic Disease Self-Management Program*, http://www.aoa.gov/AoAroot/PRESS_Room/News/2009/ 03_1 8_09.aspx, and HHS, "Secretary Sebelius Awards Funding for Chronic Disease Self-Management Programs for Older Americans," press release, March 30, 2010, http://www.hhs.gov/news/press/2010pres/03/20100330a.html.

[12] HHS, AOA, *Fiscal Year 2011 Justification of Estimates for Appropriations Committees*, pp. 93-94.

[13] Section 119 of the Medicare Improvements for Patients and Providers Act of 2008 (MIPPA, P.L. 110-275) provided $25 million for fiscal years 2008 and 2009 for these activities. Funds were allocated to State Health Insurance Programs (SHIPs), AAAs, ADRCs, and AOA. PPACA allocates the funds to SHIPs, AAAs, ADRCs, and the National Center for Benefits Outreach and Enrollment in the same proportion as under MIPPA.

[14] The 56 state agencies on aging include units in 50 states, 5 U.S. territories, and the District of Columbia. More information is at the AOA website at http://www.aoa.gov/AoARoot/AoA_Programs/OAA/Aging_Network/Index.aspx and http://www.aoa.gov/AoARoot/AoA_Programs/OAA/.

[15] State allotments for Title III programs are listed at HHS, AOA, *Funding Allocations to State and Tribal Organizations*, http://www.aoa.gov/AoARoot/AoA_ Programs/OAA/Aging_Network/State_Allocations/index.aspx.

[16] HHS, AOA, Aging Network, *Aging Integrated Database (AGID)*, 2008 State Program Reports, Total Counts: Clients Served - All Services: 50 States + DC & Territories, http://www.data.aoa.gov/.

[17] AOA has posted the state-by-state distribution of ARRA nutrition funds at http://www.aoa.gov/AoARoot/Press_Room/News/2009/DOCS/AoA_ARRA_Nutrition_Services_to_States_3-3-09.xls and http://www.hhs.gov/recovery/programs/aoa/arrafundingmap.html.

[18] HHS, AOA, *Fiscal Year 2011 Justification of Estimates for Appropriations Committees*, p. 9.

[19] U.S. Congress, House Committee on Appropriations, *The American Recovery and Reinvestment Act of 2009*, 111th Cong., 1st sess., January 26, 2009, H.Rept. 111-4 (Washington: GPO, 2009), p. 55.

[20] U.S. Congress, Senate Committee on Appropriations, *Making Supplemental Appropriations For Job Preservation And Creation, Infrastructure Investment, Energy Efficiency And Science, Assistance To The Unemployed, And State And Local Fiscal Stabilization, For The Fiscal Year Ending September 30, 2009, and for Other Purposes*, 111th Cong., 1st sess., January 27, 2009, S.Rept. 111-3 (Washington: GPO, 2009), p. 58.

[21] HHS, AOA, *Fiscal Year 2011 Justification of Estimates for Appropriations Committees*, pp. 9, 34.

[22] See "Supporting Family Caregivers," in White House Task Force on the Middle Class, *Annual Report of the White House Task Force on the Middle Class*, February 26, 2010, http://www.whitehouse.gov/sites/default/files/microsites/100226-annual-report-middle-class.pdf.

[23] HHS, AOA, *Fiscal Year 2011 Justification of Estimates for Appropriations Committees*, p. 27.

[24] HHS, AOA, *Fiscal Year 2011 Justification of Estimates for Appropriations Committees*, p. 60.

[25] AOA's estimate assumes a 3.2% inflation factor from FY20 10 to FY20 11, using the U.S. Department of Agriculture's "food away from home" inflation index. HHS, AOA, *Fiscal Year 2011 Justification of Estimates for Appropriations Committees*, p. 34.

[26] For more background on naturally occurring retirement communities, see CRS Report RL34289, *Supportive Services Programs to Naturally Occurring Retirement Communities*, by Kirsten J. Colello.

[27] A compendium of Title IV grant projects is at http://www.aoa.gov/AoARoot/Grants/Compendium/index.aspx.

[28] HHS, AOA, *Fiscal Year 2011 Justification of Estimates for Appropriations Committees*, p. 89.

[29] HHS, AOA, *Fiscal Year 2011 Justification of Estimates for Appropriations Committees*, pp. 91-92. AOA explains that CLP's goal of helping seniors avoid institutionalization can be accomplished by ADRCs and other AOA-funded services.

[30] Participants' incomes must be no greater than 125% of the federal poverty guidelines. 20 C.F.R. § 641.500.

[31] DOL, *SCSEP Frequently Asked Questions*, http://www.doleta.gov/Seniors/html_docs/docs/seniorsFAQ.cfm; DOL, *FY2011 Congressional Budget Justification, Employment and Training Administration, Community Service Employment for Older Americans*, p. CSEOA-14, http://www.dol.gov/dol/budget/2011/PDF/CBJ-2011-V1-06.pdf.

[32] There are more participants than job slots because as participants leave the program, their job slots can be filled by new participants. DOL, *FY2011 Congressional Budget Justification, Employment and Training Administration, Community Service Employment for Older Americans*, pp. CSEOA-12, CSEOA-16.

[33] For further information, see CRS Report RL3 1336, *The Older Americans Act: Programs, Funding, and 2006 Reauthorization (P.L. 109-365)*, by Carol O'Shaughnessy and Angela Napili.

[34] U.S. Congress, *Conference Report to Accompany H.R. 1*, 111th Cong., 1st sess., February 12, 2009, H.Rept. 111-16 (Washington: GPO, 2009), p. 449.

[35] DOL has posted ARRA allotments at http://www.dol.gov/recovery/2009/03/19/fbgla/DOL_Formula_Block_Grant_Allocation_03192009_1447.xlsand http://www.dol.gov/recovery/

2009/03/19/fbgla/ OL_Formula_Block_Grant_Allocation_03 192009_1447.pdf. Program year 2008 allotments were announced in U.S. Department of Labor, Employment and Training Administration, *Program Year 2008 Planning Instructions and Allotments for All SCSEP Grant Applicants*, Training and Employment Guidance Letter No. 26-07, Attachments H and I, Washington, DC, April 29, 2008, http://wdr.doleta.gov/directives. The allotments were subsequently revised in U.S. Department of Labor, Employment and Training Administration, *Program Year (PY) 2008 Revised Allotments and Due Date for All SCSEP Grant Applicants*, Training and Employment Guidance Letter No. 3 0-07, Attachment H Revised, Washington, DC, May 30, 2008, http://wdr.doleta.gov/directives/attach/TEGL30- 07.pdf.

[36] The final FY2010 amount was also larger than that proposed by the FY2010 Budget Request and by the House- passed and Senate-reported FY2010 Labor-HHS-Education Appropriations bills. For FY2010, the President had requested $575.4 million, the House bill had proposed $615.4 million, and the Senate bill had proposed $575.4 million. (H.Rept. 111-366, p. 1251).

[37] U.S. Congress, House Committee on Appropriations, *Departments of Transportation and Housing and Urban Development, and Related Agencies Appropriations Act, 2010*, Conference Report to Accompany H.R. 3288, 111$^{th}$ Cong., 1$^{st}$ sess., December 8, 2009, H.Rept. 111-366 (Washington: GPO, 2009), p. 1251.H. Rept. 111-366, p. 989.

[38] H.Rept. 111-366, p. 989. The $225 million are being prorated across two program years, 2009 ($66.176 million) and 2010 ($158.823 million). DOL, *FY2011 Congressional Budget Justification, Employment and Training Administration, Community Service Employment for Older Americans*, p. CSEOA-16. The grantees receiving the $225 million are listed in DOL, "US Department of Labor awards $225 million to Senior Community Service Employment Program grantees," press release, January 29, 2010, http://www.dol.gov/opa/media

[39] DOL, *FY2011 Congressional Budget Justification, Employment and Training Administration, Community Service Employment for Older Americans*, p. CSEOA-2.

[40] DOL, *FY2011 Congressional Budget Justification, Employment and Training Administration, Community Service Employment for Older Americans*, p. CSEOA-12.

[41] HHS, AOA, *Fiscal Year 2011 Justification of Estimates for Appropriations Committees*, p. 44.

[42] AOA has posted the distribution of ARRA nutrition funds, by tribe, at *http://transparency. nih.gov/ RecoveryGrants/tribegrant.cfm?grant=TribalNutrition*

[43] HHS, AOA, Aging Network, *Aging Integrated Database (AGID)*, National Ombudsman Reporting System, Total Counts, Cases Opened and Total Number of Complaints; Other Ombudsman Activities, Total Number of Consultations to Facilities and Individuals: 50 States + DC & Territories, http://www.data.aoa.gov/.

[44] State allocation tables are at HHS, AOA, *Fiscal Year 2011 Justification of Estimates for Appropriations Committees*, pp. 83-86.

[45] More information about the Alzheimer's Disease Support Services Program is on the AOA website at http://www.aoa.gov/AoARoot/AoA_Programs/HCLTC/Alz_Grants/index.aspx

[46] The ADDGS Program was authorized under Sections 398 to 398B of the PHSA (42 U.S.C. 280c-3 to 280c-5). Authorization of appropriations expired in 2002.

[47] More information about the Lifespan Respite Care Program is on the AOA website at http://www.aoa.gov/AoARoot/ AoA_Programs/HCLTC/LRCP/.

[48] The Lifespan Respite Care Program is authorized for $53.3 million for FY2009, $71.1 million for FY2010, and $94.8 million for FY20 11 (42 U.S.C. 300ii-4).

[49] U.S. Department of Health Education and Welfare, Special Staff on Aging, *The Nation and Its Older People, Report of the White House Conference on Aging, Jan. 9-12, 1961*, Washington, April 1961.

[50] Public Papers of the Presidents of the United States, *Lyndon B. Johnson*, vol. 2, Washington, 1965, p. 744.

In: The Older Americans Act: Provisions,... ISBN: 978-1-61122-801-4
Editor: Jamie N. Palamino ©2011 Nova Science Publishers, Inc.

*Chapter 2*

# OLDER AMERICANS ACT: TITLE III NUTRITION SERVICES PROGRAM

## *Kirsten J. Colello*

### SUMMARY

The elderly nutrition services program, authorized under Title III of the Older Americans Act, provides grants to state agencies on aging to support congregate and home-delivered meals for people aged 60 and older. The program is designed to address problems of food insecurity, promote socialization, and promote the health and well-being of older persons through nutrition and nutrition-related services. It is the largest Older Americans Act program, funded at $819.5 million in FY2010, accounting for over one-third (35%) of the Act's total funding. In FY2008, the most recent year for which data are available, over 240 million meals were served to about 2.6 million people; 61% were served to frail older people living at home, and 39% were served in congregate settings. The number of home-delivered meals served has outpaced congregate meals, growing by almost 44% from FY1990 to FY2008; the number of congregate meals served declined by 34%. The faster growth in home-delivered meals is partially due to relatively higher growth in federal funding for home-delivered meals over that time period, as well as state decisions to focus funds on frail older people living at home. Congress approved the Older Americans Act Amendments of 2006 (P.L. 109-365) extending the Act's authorization of appropriations through FY2011.

The elderly nutrition services program, authorized under Title III of the Older Americans Act (OAA)[1], provides grants to state agencies on aging to support congregate and home-Tdelivered meals to people aged 60 and older. The program is the largest component of the Act, accounting for $819.5 million, or about one-third (35%), of the Act's total FY2010 funding of $2.328 billion. The program is designed to address problems of food insecurity, promote socialization, and promote the health and well-being of older persons through nutrition and nutrition-related services. It evolved from demonstration projects first funded in 1968. In 1972, Congress authorized the program as a separate title of the Act and, in 1978, incorporated it into Title III. In 2006, Congress enacted P.L. 109-365, which reauthorized all programs under the Act through FY2011.[2]

## PURPOSE

P.L. 109-365 added a new purpose statement for the nutrition services program emphasizing both its nutritional and socialization aspects and its importance in promoting the health of older people. The purposes of the program as stipulated in the law are to (1) reduce hunger and food insecurity, (2) promote socialization of older individuals, and (3) promote the health and wellbeing of older individuals by assisting them to access nutrition and other disease prevention and health promotion services to delay the onset of adverse health conditions resulting from poor nutritional health or sedentary behavior.

## NUTRITION SERVICES PROGRAM

The Administration on Aging (AoA) in the Department of Health and Human Services (HHS) administers the Nutrition Services Program, which includes (1) the Congregate Nutrition Services Program, (2) the Home-Delivered Nutrition Services Programs, (3) and the Nutrition Services Incentive Program (NSIP). For the Congregate and Home-Delivered Programs, services must be targeted at persons with the greatest social and economic need, with particular attention to low-income older persons, including low-income minority older persons, older persons with limited English proficiency, older persons residing in rural areas, and those at risk for institutionalization. Means tests for program participation are prohibited, but older persons are encouraged to contribute to the costs of nutrition services, including meals. Older individuals may not be denied services for failure to contribute. The following describes these programs in greater detail.

## Congregate Nutrition Services

Congregate nutrition services provide meals and related nutrition services to older individuals in a variety of sites, such as senior centers, community centers, schools, and adult day care centers. Congregate nutrition service providers can also offer a variety of nutrition related services at meal sites, such as nutrition education and screening, nutrition assessment, and counseling as appropriate. The program also provides seniors with opportunities for social engagement and volunteer opportunities.

Individuals aged 60 or older and their spouses of any age may participate in the congregate nutrition program. The following groups may also receive meals: persons under age 60 with disabilities who reside in housing facilities occupied primarily by the elderly where congregate meals are served; persons with disabilities who reside at home with, and accompany, older persons to meals; and volunteers who provide services during the meal hours.

In FY2008, the most recent year for which data are available, about 4 in 10 congregate meals (39%) were served to almost two-thirds (65%) of all OAA nutrition program participants (or 94.2 million meals to almost 1.66 million meal participants).[3] (See **Figure 1**.)

## Home-Delivered Nutrition Services

Home-delivered nutrition services provide meals and related nutrition services to older individuals that are homebound. According to AoA, home-delivered meals are often the first in-home service that an older adult receives, and the program is a primary access point for other home and community-based services.[4] Like congregate nutrition service providers, home-delivered service providers can offer services such as nutrition screening and education, nutrition assessment, and counseling as appropriate. Home-delivered meals are also an important service for many family caregivers by assisting family members with their caregiving responsibilities and, for some, helping them maintain their own health and personal well-being.[5]

Individuals aged 60 or older and homebound and their spouses of any age may participate in the home-delivered nutrition program. Services may be available to individuals who are under age 60 with disabilities if they reside at home with the homebound older individual.

In FY2008, 6 in 10 meals (61%) were delivered to over one-third (35%) of all OAA nutrition program participants (or 146.4 million home-delivered meals to almost 910,000 participants).[6] (See **Figure 1**.)

## Nutrition Services Incentive Program

The Nutrition Services Incentives Program (NSIP) provides funds to states, territories, and Indian tribal organizations to purchase food or to cover the costs of food commodities provided by the U.S. Department of Agriculture (USDA) for the congregate and home-delivered nutrition programs. Originally established by the OAA in 1974 as the Nutrition Program for the Elderly in USDA,[7] Congress transferred the administration of NSIP from USDA to AoA in 2003.[8] However, states and other entities may still choose to receive all or part of their NSIP allotments in the form of commodities. Obligations for commodity procurement for NSIP are funded under an agreement between USDA and HHS.[9]

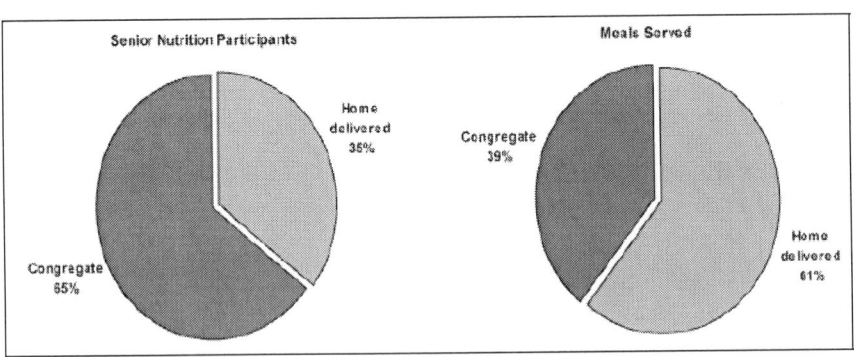

Source: CRS analysis of data from Administration on Aging, "State Program Report 2008," AGing Integrated Database at http://www.agidnet.org/.

Figure 1. Proportion of Senior Nutrition Participants and Meals Served for Congregate and Home-Delivered Nutrition Programs, FY2008

## FUNDING

The AoA awards separate allotments of funds for the congregate nutrition services program and home-delivered nutrition services program to states and territories. State agencies, in turn, award nutrition services funds to the 629 area agencies on aging that administer the program in their respective planning and service areas. The AoA also awards a separate allotment to states, territories, and Indian tribal organizations for NSIP funds.

Funds for congregate and home-delivered nutrition services are allotted to states according to a formula based on each state's relative share of the population aged 60 and over; however, the law stipulates that no state receive less than it received in FY2006. P.L. 109-365 gradually eliminated a guaranteed growth factor in the formula, beginning in FY2008.[10] States are required to provide a matching share of 15% in order to receive funds for congregate and home-delivered nutrition programs.

**Table 1. OAA Nutrition Services Program Funding, FY1990-FY2010 (2009 constant dollars, in millions)**

| Fiscal year | Congregate meals | Home-Delivered meals | NSIP | Total |
|---|---|---|---|---|
| 1990 | $576.9 | $129.5 | $235.3 | $941.7 |
| 1995 | $530.3 | $132.8 | $211.7 | $874.7 |
| 2000 | $466.4 | $183.2 | $174.4 | $824.1 |
| 2005 | $424.3 | $200.3 | $162.8 | $787.4 |
| 2006 | $408.3 | $192.7 | $156.6 | $757.7 |
| 2007 | $413.2 | $195.0 | $153.1 | $761.4 |
| 2008 | $404.0 | $190.7 | $150.9 | $745.6 |
| 2009[a] | $434.3 | $214.5 | $161.0 | $809.7 |
| 2010 | $440.8 | $217.7 | $161.0 | $819.5 |

Source: CRS analysis based on AoA/HHS and USDA amounts from appropriations legislation adjusted by the CPI-U.

a. The American Recovery and Reinvestment Act (ARRA, P.L. 111-5) appropriated additional funding for senior nutrition services. This amount is not included in the FY2009 total. Specifically, ARRA appropriated $100 million for senior nutrition services, of which $97 million was provided to states and territories ($65 million for congregate and $32 million for home-delivered meals), and $3 million was made available to Indian tribal organizations. States and territories received separate allotments for congregate nutrition and home-delivered nutrition programs based on the states population age 60 and older relative to the total U.S. population age 60 and older. For further information, see http://www.aoa.gov/AoAroot/ PRESS_Room/News/2009/03_18_09.aspx.

NSIP funds are allotted to states and other entities based on each state's share of total meals served by the nutrition services program (both congregate and home-delivered meals) in all states and tribes during the prior year. As previously mentioned, states receive their share of NSIP funds in cash, but may elect to use some or all of their funds to purchase commodities through the USDA. Most states choose to receive their share of funds in cash, rather than commodities.[11] There is no matching requirement for NSIP funds.

In FY2010, of the total $819.5 million appropriated for the program, $440.8 million was for congregate nutrition (54%), $217.7 million for home-delivered nutrition (26%), and $161.0 million for nutrition services incentive grants (20%) (Table 1).[12] Funding for nutrition services represents 60% of FY2010 funding for Title III, which also funds a wide array of social services, family caregiver support activities, and disease prevention and health promotion services for older individuals.

When adjusted for inflation, the total amount of funding appropriated for OAA Nutrition Services has decreased substantially over the past two decades ($819.5 million for FY2010 compared to $941.7 million in FY1990). This decline in relative funding has been experienced by the congregate meals and NSIP programs, while funding levels for the home-delivered meals programs have increased over the same time period.

In constant 2009 dollars, the total appropriation for congregate meals, home-delivered meals, and NSIP fell from $941.7 million in 1990 to $745.6 million in 2008, a decline of $196.1 million or 21%. The amount appropriated for congregate meals fell from $576.9 million to $404 million, a decline of $172.9 million or 30%. The amount appropriated for NSIP fell from $253.3 million to $150.9 million, a decline of $84.4 million or 36%. Only the amount appropriated for home-delivered meals increased in real terms from 1990 to 2008, rising from $129.5 million to $190.7 million, an increase of $61.2 million or 47%.

Overall, this reduction in purchasing power has affected the number of meals served, which declined by 3.9 million meals (or 2%) from FY1990 to FY2008, the most recent year for which data are available (see Table 2). The overall decline in meals served is due to a substantial decrease in the number of congregate meals served, while the number of home-delivered meals has increased.

**Table 2. OAA Nutrition Services, Number of Meals Served, FY1990-FY2008 (in millions)**

| Fiscal year | Congregate meals | Home-delivered meals | Total meals | Home-delivered meals as a percent of total meals |
|---|---|---|---|---|
| 1990 | 142.4 | 101.8 | 244.2 | 42% |
| 1995 | 123.4 | 119.0 | 242.4 | 49% |
| 2000 | 116.0 | 143.5 | 259.4 | 55% |
| 2005 | 100.5 | 140.1 | 240.6 | 58% |
| 2008 | 94.2 | 146.4 | 240.6 | 61% |

Source: Data from Administration on Aging, "State Program Report 2008," AGing Integrated Database at http://www.agidnet.org/.

Fewer congregate meals served over the past two decades can also be attributed to states transferring allotted funds from the congregate nutrition program to certain OAA Title III programs. As previously mentioned, states receive separate allotments for congregate and home-delivered nutrition services, as well as for supportive services. However, they are allowed to transfer allotted funds among these three programs (up to 40% of funds between congregate and home-delivered nutrition services allotments with waivers for higher amounts if approved by the Assistant Secretary for Aging; and up to 30% among supportive services and congregate and home-delivered nutrition services allotments). States may not transfer NSIP allotted funds among these programs.

In recent years, state transfer of funds has resulted in a decrease of funds available for congregate nutrition services. In FY2008, states transferred $77.8 million out of their congregate nutrition services allotments to either the home-delivered nutrition or supportive services allotments. These funding transfers resulted in a decrease of 19.2% in funds that were originally allotted to states for the congregate program. Funds available for home-delivered meals increased by 19.9% as a result of funding transfers. Funds for the supportive services program increased by 11.4%.[13] State initiatives to respond to the demand for home-based services by frail homebound older persons is an important factor in their decisions to transfer funds.

## SERVICE DELIVERY REQUIREMENTS

Congregate and home-delivered nutrition services providers are required to offer at least one meal per day, five or more days per week (except in rural areas where less frequency is allowed). Meals provided must comply with the Dietary Guidelines for Americans published by the Secretary of HHS and the Secretary of Agriculture. Providers must serve meals that meet certain dietary requirements based on the number of meals served by the project each day. Providers that serve one meal per day must provide to each participant a minimum of one-third of the daily recommended dietary reference intakes (DRIs) established by the Food and Nutrition Board of the Institute of Medicine (IOM). Providers that serve two meals per day must provide a minimum of two-thirds of the DRIs, and those that serve three meals per day must provide 100% of the DRIs. Providers must provide meals that comply with state or local laws regarding safe and sanitary handling of food, equipment, and supplies that are used to store, prepare and deliver meals, and must carry out meal programs using the advice of dietitians and meal participants. The law requires providers to offer nutrition screening and education to participants, and where appropriate, nutrition assessment and counseling. Providers are encouraged to make arrangements with schools and other facilities serving meals to children in order to promote intergenerational meals programs.

P.L. 109-365 noted that while diet is the preferred source of nutrition, evidence suggests that the use of a single daily multivitamin-mineral supplement may be an effective way to address poor nutrition among older people. Also, it noted that Title III nutrition service providers should consider whether congregate and home-delivered participants would benefit from a multivitamin-mineral supplement that is in compliance with government quality standards and that provides at least two-thirds of essential vitamins and minerals at 100% of daily value levels as determined by the Commissioner of Food and Drugs.[14]

## MEALS SERVED

In FY2008, almost 241 million meals were provided to older people (see Table 2). In FY1990, home-delivered meals represented 42% of total meals served, but by FY2008, the share had climbed to 61% of total meals. From

1990 to 2008, the number of home-delivered meals served grew by almost 44%, while the number of congregate meals served actually declined by 34%. A number of reasons account for this, including the trend by states to transfer funds from their congregate services allotments to home-delivered services; greater growth in federal funding for home-delivered services relative to the congregate nutrition program funds; state initiatives to expand home care services for frail older persons; and successful leveraging of non-federal funds for home-delivered services.

AoA data show that for FY2008, the U.S. average expenditure for congregate meals was $6.75, ranging from $15.94 in Alaska to $1.55 in Puerto Rico. The average expenditure for home-delivered meals was $5.14, ranging from $11.72 in Wyoming to $1.46 in Puerto Rico.[15]

## PROGRAM PARTICIPATION

A 2008 National Survey of OAA participants show that in 2008, 60% of congregate nutrition survey respondents were age 75 and older; 48% lived alone; 16% had annual income of $10,000 or less; and 58% reported that the congregate meals program provided one-half or more of their daily food intake. Furthermore, many congregate nutrition recipients reported these meals have fostered greater socialization, with 82% saying that they see friends more often due to meals.[16]

This 2008 survey found that 71% of home-delivered respondents were age 75 and older; 60% lived alone; 28% had annual income of $10,000 or less; and 60% said that the home-delivered meals program provided at least one-half of their daily food intake. According to the survey, home-delivered meals recipients are particularly frail and are at risk for institutionalization. Almost 40% of recipients reported needing assistance with one or more activities of daily living (ADLs, such as bathing, dressing, eating, and using the toilet); 14% of these recipients needed assistance with three or more ADLs. In addition, 84% reported needing assistance with one or more instrumental activities of daily living (IADLs, such as shopping, telephoning, housework, and getting around inside the home).[17]

## PROGRAM EVALUATION

The last major national evaluation of the nutrition program was completed in 1996. It showed that, compared to the total elderly population, nutrition program participants were older and more likely to be poor, to live alone, and to be members of minority groups. Almost half of home-delivered meal recipients and more than one-third of congregate meal recipients had income below the federal poverty level, compared to about 15% of the total U.S. population age 60 and over (at the time of the evaluation). Recipients were also more likely to have health and functional limitations that place them at nutritional risk. The report found the program plays an important role in participants' overall nutrition and that meals consumed by participants are their primary source of daily nutrients. The evaluation also found that the program leverages a fairly significant amount of nonfederal dollars: for every federal dollar spent, the program leveraged (at that time) on average $1.70 for congregate meals, and $3.35 for home-delivered meals from a variety of sources, including state, local, and private funds as well as participant contributions toward the cost of meals.[18]

The 2006 reauthorization legislation stipulated that the Institute of Medicine (IOM) conduct an evidence-based study of the program. The study is to include (1) an evaluation of the effect of nutrition projects on the health and nutrition status of participants, prevention of hunger and food insecurity, and ability of participants to remain living independently; (2) a cost-benefit analysis of nutrition projects, including their potential to affect Medicaid costs; and (3) recommendations on how nutrition projects may be modified to improve outcomes, and the nutritional quality of meals. To date, AoA has not conducted this study. However, prior to the 2006 reauthorization AoA had begun the process to conduct a new evaluation of the Title III Nutrition Services Program. According to AoA, this evaluation will contain (1) an evaluation of program impacts on participants' nutrition, health and well-being, socialization, and food insecurity; (2) a cost analysis that describes the cost per meal by cost categories and method of meal production; and (3) a process evaluation that examines the implementation of the program at the state and local levels and includes an assessment of the nutritional quality of the program meals.[19] The participant outcomes component will involve a matched comparison group and similar survey methods as those used in the National Health and Nutrition Examination Study (NHANES) to allow for comparison of research results to the previous evaluation, a matched comparison group, and national estimates from NHANES and other national data.

## ACKNOWLEDGMENTS

This report updates a report that was previously authored by Carol O'Shaughnessy.

## End Notes

[1] 42 U.S.C. 3021 et. seq. Regulations are at 45 C.F.R. 1321.1 et. seq.
[2] For further information, see CRS Report RL31336, *The Older Americans Act: Programs, Funding, and 2006 Reauthorization (P.L. 109-365)*, by Carol O'Shaughnessy and Angela Napili.
[3] Data from Administration on Aging, "State Program Report 2008," AGing Integrated Database at http://www.agidnet.org/.
[4] Administration on Aging, "Nutrition Services (Title C)," at http://www.aoa.gov/AoARoot/AoA_Programs/HCLTC/Nutrition_Services/index.aspx.
[5] For further information on family caregiving, see CRS Report RL34123, *Family Caregiving to the Older Population: Background, Federal Programs, and Issues for Congress*, by Kirsten J. Colello.
[6] Data from Administration on Aging, "State Program Report 2008," AGing Integrated Database at http://www.agidnet.org/.
[7] The program was originally established for commodities only. In 1977, states could receive allotments from USDA in cash or commodities.
[8] Division G, Title II, Section 217 of the Consolidated Appropriations Resolution, 2003 (P.L. 108-7).
[9] In 2006, pursuant to P.L. 109-365, Congress rescinded states' option to receive commodities. However, in 2007, this option was reinstated through P.L. 110-19 (effective April 23, 2007) which authorized the transfer of NSIP funds from HHS to USDA for the purchase of commodities and related expenses.
[10] For further information, see CRS Report RS22549, *Older Americans Act: Funding Formulas*, by Kirsten J. Colello.
[11] In FY2008, 8 states chose to receive a portion of their share of the nutrition services incentive funds in commodities: Connecticut, Delaware, Idaho, Kansas, Massachusetts, Montana, Nevada, and Oklahoma. The FY2008 value for these commodities was $2.7 million.
[12] For further information on OAA funding, see CRS Report RL33880, *Older Americans Act (OAA) Funding*, by Angela Napili. For information on state funding allocations see http://www.aoa.gov/AoARoot/AoA_Programs/OAA/Aging_Network/State_Allocations/.
[13] Data from Administration on Aging, "2008 U.S. Profile of OAA Programs," obtained through personal communication from the Administration on Aging, November 17, 2009.
[14] Section 318 of P.L. 109-365.
[15] Data from Administration on Aging, "State Program Report 2008," AGing Integrated Database at http://www.agidnet.org/.
[16] Data from Administration on Aging, "National Survey of OAA Participants, 2008," AGing Integrated Database at http://www.agidnet.org/.

[17] Ibid.

[18] U.S. Department of Health and Human Services, Office of the Assistant Secretary for Aging, *Serving Elders at Risk: The Older Americans Act Nutrition Programs*, National Evaluation of the Elderly Nutrition Program, 1993-1995, June 1996. Available at http://www.aoa.dhhs.gov/prof/aoaprog/nutrition/program_eval/eval_report.asp, visited Feb. 5, 2007.

[19] The evaluation is being conducted by Mathematica Policy, Inc. Data collection is planned for 2010 and 2011 with results reported in 2012. Personal communication from the Administration on Aging, November 17, 2009.

*Chapter 3*

# OLDER AMERICANS ACT: PRELIMINARY OBSERVATIONS ON SERVICES REQUESTED BY SENIORS AND CHALLENGES IN PROVIDING ASSISTANCE

### *Kay E. Brown*

#### WHY GAO DID THIS STUDY

Administered by the Administration on Aging (AoA) in the Department of Health and Human Services (HHS), Title III of the Older Americans Act (OAA) is intended to assist individuals age 60 and older by providing supportive services. Title III, Medicaid and Medicare, state, and other sources of funding provide for several types of services, including congregate and home-delivered meals, transportation, and support for caregivers.

This testimony reports on ongoing GAO work in preparation for the reauthorization of the OAA and a full report to be issued by GAO in 2011. Based on preliminary findings, GAO describes (1) Title III services most requested by seniors and how state and local agencies reach those most in need, and (2) how agencies have coped with increasing requests in the current economic environment.

To do this, GAO reviewed aging plans from the 50 states and District of Columbia; conducted site visits to 4 states; interviewed national, state, and local officials; and analyzed preliminary responses to a Web-based survey of 125 Local Area Agencies on Aging for fiscal year 2009. The survey data used in this document reflect a 54 percent response rate as of July 30, 2010. The survey is still in progress and our results are not generalizable at this time. GAO shared its findings with AoA and incorporated their comments as appropriate.

## WHAT GAO FOUND

Seniors frequently requested home-delivered meals and transportation services, and based on preliminary responses to GAO's survey and information from site visits, demand for some Title III services may be increasing. Some agencies said they were unable to meet all requests for services in fiscal year 2009. For example, 13 of 67 survey respondents said they were generally or very unable to serve all seniors who requested home-delivered meals, and 15 of 63 said they were generally or very unable to serve all who requested transportation assistance. Local officials cite seniors' desire to remain in their homes as they age, and the economic downturn as possible reasons for increased requests. Given this demand, providers must make decisions about which applicants will receive services. OAA requires providers to target those with the greatest economic and social need,—low-income, minority, lacking proficiency in English, and rural residents—and local officials said they advertise, conduct outreach, and coordinate with other local organizations to identify and serve these groups. Additionally, most local agencies reported screening potential clients to assess level of need, for example, to determine those most at risk of hospitalization due to poor nutrition. In addition to these known service needs, an unknown number of other seniors may need services but not know to contact OAA providers, some officials told GAO.

Local agencies who responded to GAO's survey reported using the flexibility afforded by the OAA to transfer funds among Title III programs to meet increased requests for specific services. Twenty-eight of 61 local agencies said they transferred funds in fiscal year 2009, most often removing funds from congregate meals to home-delivered meals or other services. Although the American Recovery and Reinvestment Act (Recovery Act) provided an additional $97 million specifically for meal programs, Title III programs are heavily reliant on state funds, and 44 of 64 local agencies responding to our survey said their state funding was reduced for fiscal year 2010. To cope with funding reductions, some reported cutting services to seniors. Twenty-seven of 65 local agencies said they cut administrative expenses in fiscal year 2010; others relocated offices or left agency positions vacant. Some state and local officials said they provided less service to individuals so that more could get some amount of assistance. Some agencies said they used Recovery Act funds to replace lost state and local funding or created new programs, but the funding was restricted to meal services and was a relatively small percentage of total OAA allocations.

The proportion of Americans age 60 and over will continue to grow over the coming decades, and demand for Title III services also will likely grow. Therefore it will be increasingly important for service providers to focus services on those most in need.

Mr. Chairman:

Thank you for inviting me here today to discuss the preliminary results of our work that you requested on services and funding provided under the Older Americans Act of 1965 (OAA).[1] Title III of OAA provides for a broad range of home- and community-based services for older Americans and their caregivers, including providing meals, transportation, assistance with personal care and housekeeping, and time off (respite) for seniors' caregivers. About 10 million seniors age 60 and older, or about 18 percent of the national 60 and over population, benefited from these programs in fiscal year 2008, the most current year for which these data were available. In fiscal year 2009, Congress provided $1.2 billion for grants to states for home- and community-based services under Title III of the OAA.[2] Future funding will be determined in the reauthorization process in 2011.

Demographic studies show that older Americans will make up a larger proportion of the country's population in coming decades, with those aged 65 and older projected to increase from 40 million in 2010 to 72 million in 2030.[3] Delivery of services related to long-term care, nutrition, and other needs of seniors will likely be increasingly in demand as well, particularly services that help individuals remain in their homes and communities.

Currently, an economic downturn has challenged many seniors' ability to meet basic needs as well as the resources of agencies that provide assistance. The American Recovery and Reinvestment Act of 2009 (Recovery Act)[4] provided a one-time addition of $97 million for Title III home-delivered and congregate meals for seniors. The Administration on Aging (AoA) requires states to expend these funds by December 30, 2010.

For today's testimony, we focused on the following questions: (1) Which Title III services are most requested, and how do state and local agencies reach those seniors most in need? (2) How have agencies coped with increasing requests in the current economic environment?

Our analysis is based on preliminary responses to a GAO Web-based survey of a random national sample of 125 local area agencies on aging.[5] As of July 30, 2010, our response rate was 54 percent. These agencies are the frontline administrators of Title III services for seniors, and our survey asked them about fiscal year 2009. We also reviewed 51 aging plans from states and the District of Columbia, reviewed relevant statutory provisions, conducted site visits to 4 states, and interviewed national, state, and local officials involved in Title III programs. This testimony is part of ongoing work for a report requested by the Special Committee on Aging and scheduled to be issued in early 2011 in which we intend to estimate need for and potential gaps in Title III services, and provide results from our completed survey. We discussed our preliminary results with AoA and incorporated their comments as appropriate. For more information on our scope and methodology, see appendix I.

We conducted this performance audit from December 2009 to August 2010, in accordance with generally accepted government auditing standards. Those standards require that we plan and perform the audit to obtain sufficient, appropriate evidence to provide a reasonable basis for our findings and conclusions based on our audit objectives. We believe that the evidence obtained provides a reasonable basis for our findings and conclusions.

## BACKGROUND

The purpose of Title III of the OAA is to help seniors maintain independence in their homes and communities by providing appropriate support services and promoting a continuum of care for the vulnerable elderly.[6] The OAA laid the foundation for the current aging services network. This network is comprised of 56 state units on aging (SUA), 629 area agencies on aging (AAA), 244 tribal and Native American organizations, and 2 organizations serving Native Hawaiians, as well as nearly 20,000 local service provider organizations.[7] These organizations are responsible for the planning, development, and coordination of a wide array of home and community-based services within each state under Title III of the OAA. This testimony focuses on three categories of services—those provided under parts B, C, and E of Title III of the OAA. Part B covers, among other things, supportive services and senior centers, including transportation, help with homemaker tasks and personal care, and adult day care.[8] Part C covers nutrition services, including home-delivered and congregate meals.[9] Part E authorizes the National Family Caregiver Support Program, which provides counseling, support groups, and relief from caregiver duties (respite services) for caregivers.[10] (See table 1.)

**Table 1. OAA Expenditures on Title III Services, Parts B, C, and E, FY 2008**

| (Dollars in millions) | |
|---|---|
| Select services provided through OAA Title III | OAA Title III expenditures[a] by service |
| **Part B: Support (Assistance) Services** | |
| Other services | $105.5 |
| Transportation | 68.0 |
| Information and assistance[b] | 53.2 |
| Case management | 34.4 |
| Homemaker | 27.1 |
| Legal assistance | 24.8 |
| Personal care | 12.7 |
| Adult day care/Health | 11.8 |
| Outreach | 11.4 |
| Chore[c] | 5.8 |
| Assisted transportation | 3.7 |
| **Part C: Nutrition Services** | |
| Congregate meals | 265.5 |
| Home-delivered meals | 228.2 |
| Nutrition education | 3.5 |
| Nutrition counseling | 1.0 |
| **Part E: Caregiver Services** | |
| Respite care | 55.1 |
| Access assistance[d] | 30.9 |
| Counseling/support groups/caregiver training | 15.9 |
| Supplemental services[e] | 14.1 |
| Information services[f] | 13.6 |

Source: State Program Reports Data from the Administration on Aging's AGIntegrated Database (AGID) - http://www.agidnet.org/ (last accessed Jan. 29, 2010).

[a] Expenditures for the 50 states, District of Columbia, and U.S. territories.

[b] Information and assistance refers to brochures, literature, and information provided to seniors and care givers about services, programs and resources they may wish to access.

c Chore services includes assistance with heavy housework, yard work, or sidewalk maintenance.
d Access assistance refers to assistance to caregivers in locating services from a variety of private and voluntary agencies.
e Supplemental services are provided on a limited basis to complement the care provided by caregivers. Home modifications, assistive technologies, and emergency response systems are examples of supplemental services.
f Information services refers to information given to caregivers about available services within their communities.

AoA at the Department of Health and Human Services provides grants to the states through the SUAs. Grant amounts are based on funding formulas weighted to reflect a state's age 60 and over population, which is generally the group eligible for services.[11] For example, in fiscal year 2009, the state of Florida received about $87 million in Title III dollars compared to the state of Montana, which received $6 million, because more seniors reside in Florida. SUAs then typically allocate funds to Area Agencies on Aging (AAA) to directly provide services or to contract with local service providers. In a few states, the SUA directly allocates funds to local providers or provides services. (See figure 1.)

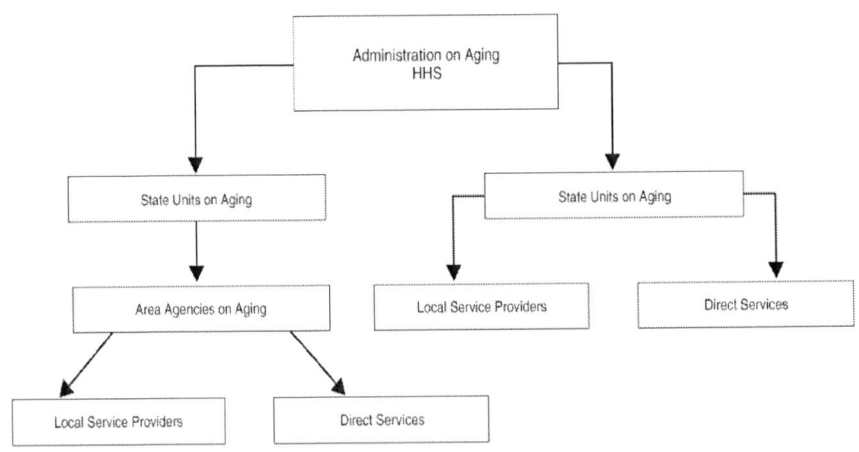

Source: GAO.

Figure 1. Flow of Title III Funds

A significant amount of program funding is also provided to state and local agencies by other sources, such as federal Medicare and Medicaid, states, private donations, and voluntary contributions from seniors for services they receive. According to a 2009 study published by the National Association of Area Agencies on Aging and Scripps Gerontology Center of Miami University, 99 percent of AAAs secure funds from additional sources, and the average AAA utilized funding from six sources to provide services in their communities.[12] The amount secured by AAAs varies.

OAA services are available to all people age 60 and older who need assistance. The law did not, however, establish an open-ended entitlement available to all seniors, nor was it intended to meet all of seniors' needs. OAA requires providers to target, or place a priority on reaching, seniors with the greatest economic and social need, and defines them as individuals who have an income at or below the poverty level, or who are culturally, socially, or geographically isolated, face language barriers, or have physical and mental disabilities.[13] Targeting these seniors who are most in need may include a local agency locating a congregate meal site in a low-income neighborhood or working collaboratively with organizations that represent minority seniors. In addition, some services are targeted to vulnerable groups by definition. Examples of these include the long-term care ombudsman program, family care-giver support services, and assisted transportation to those with limited mobility. OAA gives state and local agencies flexibility in determining which populations to target.

The recent health care reform legislation—the Patient Protection and Affordable Care Act—contains new provisions for senior health care, including one removing barriers to home- and community-based services under Medicaid.[14] While these changes may shift the provision of some services for seniors from OAA to Medicaid, the extent of this shift is unknown; nevertheless, seniors will likely continue to look to OAA-funded providers for a range of assistance.

## AGENCIES REPORT INCREASED REQUESTS FOR MEALS AND TRANSPORTATION AND VARIED EFFORTS TO REACH THOSE MOST IN NEED

Local agencies who responded to our survey identified home-delivered meals and transportation as frequently requested services in fiscal year 2009. These agencies also said they receive many requests for information and assistance services—help locating resources and programs—and for respite for caregivers. In preliminary responses to our survey, 49 of those 61[15] local agencies said more seniors requested home-delivered meals than congregate meals. Forty-four of our 67 survey respondents thus far cited transportation and 43 cited information and assistance as the support services requested most frequently.[16] One local official we spoke with in Wisconsin highlighted the importance of transportation services for his rural clients,[17] while an agency official in Massachusetts said OAA transportation services can be important in urban settings because seniors often prefer them to mass transit options.[18] In addition, 36 of the 63 local agencies who have responded to our survey and track such requests said respite services were most frequently requested by caregivers in fiscal year 2009. Respite care provides temporary caregiving for seniors so that a family member can take a break or engage in other activities.

Some agencies responding to our survey said they are currently unable to meet all requests for services. Thirteen of 67 agencies said they are generally or very unable to serve all clients who request home-delivered meals; 15 of the 63 agencies that provide transportation services said they are generally or very unable to meet all transportation requests. Of the 64 agencies that provide respite care, 17 said they were generally or very unable to meet all requests.

State and local officials we spoke with also said requests for some OAA services are increasing. Specifically, officials at several local agencies we visited described increased requests for home-delivered meals, transportation, or home-based services.[19] Officials attributed these increases to several factors. First, some agency officials said there are increasing numbers of Americans who are age 60 and older and eligible for services. According to U.S. Census data, more than 9 million more Americans were 60 years and older in 2009 than in 2000, and the Census Bureau projects that population group will continue to grow. Secondly, some agency officials told us requests for OAA services such as home-delivered meals and home-based care are increasing as more seniors stay in their homes longer rather than move to assisted living facilities or nursing homes.[20] For example, state officials in Wisconsin said their client population is increasingly older and those who remain in their homes less likely to go out, leading many to request home-delivered meals.

Lastly, most agencies who responded to our survey said requests for services have increased since the economic downturn began. Forty-eight of 61 said they have received increased requests for home-delivered meals, 44 of 62 for support services such as transportation, and 40 of 61 agencies for caregiver services since the downturn began. Twenty-five of 60 agencies said they had increased requests for congregate meals, even as long-term trends show a decline in use of this service.[21] A survey conducted by the National

Association of State Units on Aging to determine the impact of the economic crisis on state-provided services also found requests for the types of services provided by OAA increased, particularly for home-delivered meals, transportation, and personal care.[22] Some researchers have concluded that older Americans have been hard hit by the economic recession for reasons such as depreciating home values and retirement accounts.[23] These increasing economic challenges may lead to increased need for services like those provided by OAA programs.

Given the number of agencies that cannot meet all requests for services and the increasing demand for certain services, agencies must make decisions about which applicants to serve. To reach and serve seniors with the greatest economic or social need, local agencies responding to our survey reported a range of strategies. Over 50 of 67 agencies said they advertise, conduct outreach, and coordinate with other local organizations to reach and provide services to seniors who are targeted by OAA: seniors who are low-income, minority, or live in rural areas. At least 47 of 67 said they use these approaches to reach seniors who speak limited English, another group targeted by OAA. Additionally, most local agencies reported screening potential clients to assess, whether seniors requesting home-delivered meals or respite care had physical limitations that made these types of services particularly beneficial. For example, at one local agency where demand often exceeds supply, an official said preference may be given to those most at risk for hospitalization due to diagnosed malnutrition or chronic diseases managed through nutrition, such as diabetes. Most local agencies did not screen for congregate meals or transportation services.

Some officials we spoke to said there are additional seniors who need services but do not contact OAA providers to request them. For example, one local official in Illinois said needs assessments and anecdotal information indicate a much greater need for services than requests to the agency indicate. Similarly, researchers from one organization we spoke with surmised that if more seniors knew about the types of services available through Title III, the requests for such services would be greater. [24]

# AGENCIES OFTEN MOVE FUNDS AMONG PROGRAMS TO MEET REQUESTS AND CUT COSTS TO COPE WITH REDUCED FUNDING

Local agencies have adopted a number of coping mechanisms to address seniors' requests and decreased funding. Preliminary responses to our survey indicate agencies utilize the flexibility provided by the OAA to transfer funds among Title III programs to meet requests from seniors for services.[25] Twenty-eight of 61 local agencies responding to our question said they transferred funds among programs in fiscal year 2009, most often removing funds from congregate meals, which are less requested, to home-delivered meals or other services. On a national level, nearly 20 percent of OAA funding for congregate meals in fiscal year 2008 was transferred out of the program by states and split almost evenly between home-delivered meals and support services, AoA data show. (See figure 2.)[26] As a result, support services and home-delivered meal programs experienced an 11 percent and 20 percent net increase, respectively, in Title III funds. On the state level, 34 states transferred funds from congregate meals to home-delivered meals in fiscal year 2008, according to AoA data.

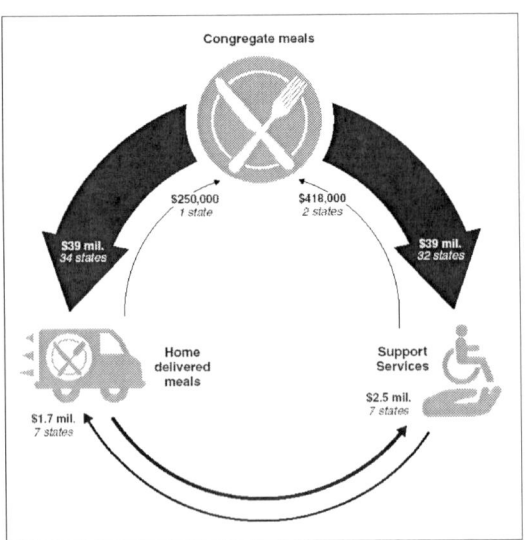

Source: GAO analysis of AoA Fiscal Year 2008 State Program Reports.

Figure 2. Fund Transfers among Title III Programs, Fiscal Year 2008

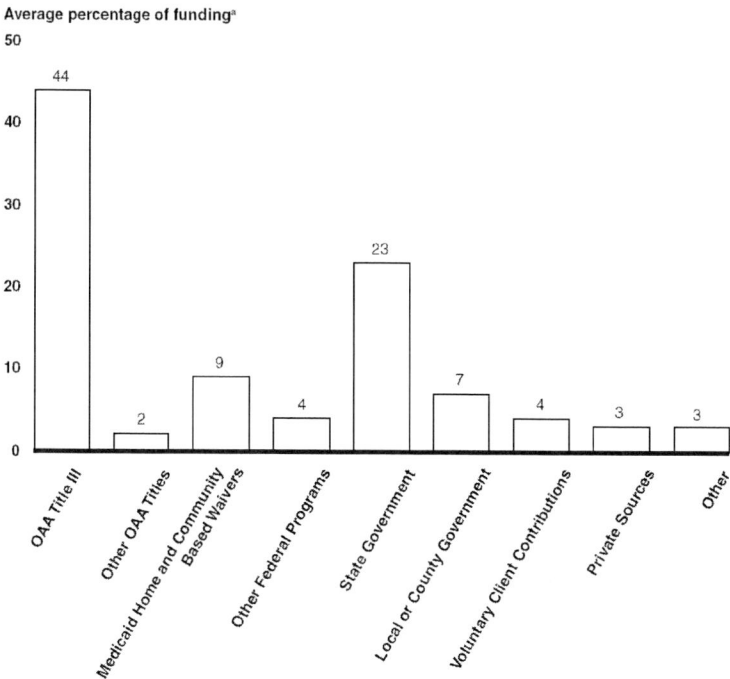

Source: GAO analysis of preliminary survey data from 58 local agencies.

Figure 3. Percentage of Funds from Various Sources, as Reported by 58 Local Agencies, Fiscal Year 2009 (Preliminary Data)

The ability to transfer funds offers states flexibility, yet some officials have questioned the need for meal funding to arrive in two streams. For example, Wisconsin state officials said maintaining separate funding for congregate and home-delivered meals creates a cumbersome process in which the state has to deal with multiple rules to allocate funds to services that are most needed. Similarly, Rhode Island state officials said they would like to see a single Title III, Part C, meal program because requests for congregate meals have decreased. In addition, in fiscal year 2008, 32 states transferred funds from the congregate meal program to Title III, Part B, services such as personal care, homemaker assistance, and transportation services. Local officials in Wisconsin told us federal funding for Part B services is not sufficient to meet requests.

In addition to receiving federal funding, the programs created by Title III of OAA receive funding from other sources as well. (See figure 3.) OAA funds to states and local agencies increased in fiscal year 2009 by $97 million due to Recovery Act funding explicitly for meal programs. But many of the local agencies responding to our survey reported overall decreases in funding from fiscal year 2009 to fiscal year 2010. Forty-four of 64 local agencies said state funding – the second largest source of funding for these programs nationally—decreased for fiscal year 2010. This is consistent with information reported by the National Association of State Units on Aging (NASUA). NASUA found that most states reported state budget shortfalls in fiscal year 2010 and reduced budgets for aging services. Local agencies also use funds from local governments, voluntary client contributions, and private sources, and our preliminary survey results indicate these funds also declined in fiscal year 2010.

Some local agencies responding to our survey reported reducing services as a result of funding cuts. Twelve of 64 local agencies said they reduced support services, an additional 12 of 63 reported reducing nutrition services, and 9 of 64 reported reducing caregiver services.

To replace lost state and local monies and maintain service levels to seniors, just under half of those responding to our survey said they took some steps to reduce administrative and operations costs and used Recovery Act funds to fill budgeting gaps. In our preliminary survey results, 27 of 65 agencies reported cutting administrative expenses, 22 of 54 reported cutting capital expenses, and 26 of 62 reported cutting operating expenditures in fiscal year 2010. Local agencies responding to our survey said they cut expenses in many ways such as by relocating to a smaller building with lower overhead costs, stretching meal service supplies, decreasing travel expenses, and limiting raises for employees. Additionally, 29 of 63 said they did not fill vacant positions. These preliminary survey data are consistent with what we heard from state officials on our site visits. State officials in Wisconsin, for example, told us that as a result of the state's budget deficit, the agency was unable to fill vacant positions and had cut planning, administration, and monitoring activities in order to avoid cutting services to seniors. Illinois state officials told us the last budget cycle included a 10 percent decrease in state funds for aging services, and there were layoffs, required furlough days, and positions left vacant as a result.

Some state and local agencies we visited also told us they adapt to limited funding or increased requests for services by providing less service to all rather than full service to only some. For example, a local official in Massachusetts said that some seniors are given fewer transit rides so others can be accommodated. A state official in Illinois said some local areas resolve the funding shortfalls by reducing the number of hours they provide respite services for each caregiver.

Local agencies said they used Recovery Act funds to fill meal budget gaps or to expand existing nutrition programs or create new ones. Nationwide, the Recovery Act provided $65 million for congregate meals and $32 million for home-delivered meals, or about 13 percent of the total OAA allocation for meals in fiscal year 2009.[27] Unlike regular Title III meal funds, Recovery Act meal funds could not be transferred among programs. Thirty-nine of 61 local agencies said it was moderately to extremely challenging that Recovery Act funds could not be transferred among meal programs.

Many local agencies responding to our survey said they used Recovery Act funds to replace funds lost from other sources; 35 of 52 local agencies said they used Recovery Act funds to expand existing nutrition programs. Fourteen of 43 local agencies said they used Recovery Act congregate meal funds to create new programs and 6 of 37 used Recovery Act home-delivered meal funds to do so. City of Chicago officials said that they used excess congregate meal funds to create a new breakfast program since they could not transfer the funds to their home-delivered meal program. But many of those responding to our survey expressed concerns about how expenses covered by Recovery Act funds will be met when the funding ends. Fifty of 61 local agencies said sustaining services currently paid with Recovery Act funds will be a moderate to extreme challenge. A local agency director in Wisconsin told us Recovery Act funds helped replace lost state funds and delayed a blow to nutrition programs which is now expected to hit in fall 2010 after the funds are spent. City of Chicago officials expressed concern about their ability to maintain their new breakfast program.

## CONCLUDING OBSERVATIONS

OAA Title III programs are an invaluable support mechanism for many seniors, providing a varied network of care and services as they age. Seniors' needs for the types of services provided through these programs will only increase over time since demographic studies show a larger proportion of Americans will be age 60 and older over the next few decades. Programs that allow seniors to remain in their own homes and communities afford seniors the independence and dignity they desire. As current fiscal stress and looming deficits continue to constrain available resources, it will be increasingly important for all elements of the home and community-based service network to focus services on those in greatest need.

Mr. Chairman, this concludes my prepared statement. I will be happy to answer any questions you may have.

## APPENDIX I: OBJECTIVES, SCOPE, AND METHODOLOGY

To determine the Title III services requested most often, local agencies' use of federal funds, and steps agencies take to deliver resources to those most in need, we conducted a web-based random national sample survey of 125 Area Agencies on Aging (AAA). The survey included questions about: (1) utilization of OAA Title III services, (2) requests for OAA Title III services, (3) approaches for measuring unmet need to target resources to areas of greatest need, (4) use of OAA Title III funds, and (5) the economic climate and use of American Recovery and Reinvestment Act (Recovery Act) funds. We drew a simple random sample of 125 agencies, from a pool of 638 agencies. This included all 629 area agencies on aging (AAA) that operate in the 50 states and District of Columbia, as well as nine State Units on Aging (SUA) in states that do not have AAAs. We included these nine state agencies in our pool for sample selection because the SUA performs the function of AAAs in those states. We conducted four pretests to help ensure that survey questions were clear, terminology was used correctly, the information could be obtained, and the survey was unbiased. Agencies were selected for pre-testing to ensure we had a group of agencies with varying operating structures, budget sizes, and geographic regions of the country. As a result of our pretests, we revised survey questions as appropriate. In June 2010, we notified the 125 AAAs that were selected to complete our survey and e-mailed a link to complete the Web survey to these agencies beginning July 1, 2010. The survey is on-going, and the information included in this testimony presents preliminary results, based on the 67 responses (54 percent) we received as of July 30, 2010. Some individual questions have lower response rates. The practical difficulties of conducting any survey may introduce nonsampling errors. For example, difficulties in interpreting a particular question, sources of information available to respondents, or entering data into a database or analyzing them can introduce unwanted variability into the survey results. We took steps in developing the questionnaire to minimize such nonsampling error. Due to the preliminary nature of the results, the information presented in this testimony is not intended to be generalizable to all AAAs.

We also reviewed relevant statutory provisions and used site visit interviews and Administration on Aging (AoA) State Program Report data to answer our two research questions. In March 2010, we visited Illinois, Massachusetts, Rhode Island, and Wisconsin. These states were selected due to varying sizes of the population age 60 and over and Title III expenditures. Additionally, we considered geographic region, proximity to AoA regional support centers, and a desire to interview at least one state without AAAs (Rhode Island). We interviewed officials from the SUA, AAAs, and AoA regional support centers. We also analyzed AoA State Program Report data available on the agency's Web site and at www.agidnet.org. We assessed the validity and reliability of this data by interviewing AoA officials, assessing official's responses to a set of standard data reliability questions, and reviewing internal documents used to edit and check data submitted by states. We determined the data were sufficiently reliable for purposes of this review.

To determine steps agencies take to deliver resources to those most in need, we also analyzed the most recently available state aging plan for the 50 states and District of Columbia. Each state is required to submit a state aging plan to AoA for review and approval covering a two, three, or four year period. The aging plan should include state long-term care reform efforts with an emphasis on home and community-based services, strategies the state employs to address the growing number of seniors, and priorities, innovations and progress the state seeks to achieve in addressing the challenges posed by an aging society.

## GAO CONTACT AND STAFF ACKNOWLEDGMENTS

For future contact regarding this testimony, please contact Kay Brown at (202) 512-7215 or e-mail brownke@gao.gov. Key contributors to this testimony were Kimberley M. Granger-Heath, Susan Aschoff, James Bennett, Ramona Burton, Andrea Dawson, Justin Fisher, Luann Moy, Barbara Steel-Lowney, and Craig Winslow.

# End Notes

[1] Pub. L. No. 89-73, 79 Stat. 219 (codified as amended at 42 U.S.C. §§ 3001 - 3058ee). It was most recently reauthorized by the Older Americans Act Amendments of 2006, Pub. L. No. 109-365, 120 Stat. 2522.

[2] Services funded through the OAA are not entitlements. The number of clients served is limited by available funding, and funding from OAA funds make up about one-third or less of total funding for services, which are delivered by state and local providers. Other funding sources include Medicaid, Medicare, state government, Social Services block grants, and voluntary contributions and donations.

[3] Population Division, U.S. Census Bureau; table 2, Projections of the Population by Selected Age Groups and Sex for the United States: 2010 to 2050 (NP2008-T2). Released August 14, 2008.

[4] Pub. L. No. 111-5, 123 Stat. 115, 179 (2010).

[5] Because the survey is still in progress and the desired response rate had not been achieved by September 1, 2010, as we prepared for today's testimony, our results are not generalizeable at this time. Our full report is to include final survey results intended to be generalizeable.

[6] 42 U.S.C. § 3021.

[7] The 56 SUAs include states, the District of Columbia, Puerto Rico, and 4 territories.

[8] 42 U.S.C. § 3030d.

[9] 42 U.S.C. §§ 3030e – 3030g-22.

[10] 42 U.S.C. §§ 3030s-3030s-2.

[11] 42 U.S.C. § 3024.

[12] *Area Agencies on Aging: Advancing Access for Home and Community-Based Services, 2008 Area Agencies on Aging Survey*, National Association of Area Agencies on Aging and Scripps Gerontology Center of Miami University (June 2009).

[13] 42 U.S.C. § 3025(a)(1)(E) and (2)(C) and (E).

[14] Pub. L. No. 111-148, § 2402, 124 Stat. 119, 301-04. Medicaid law already authorized waivers under which states could, if certain conditions were met, cover most home and community based services under Medicaid. 42 U.S.C. § 1396n(c).

[15] At the time of this testimony, 67 local agencies had responded to our survey. Because not all respondents answer every question, the numbers of total responses vary from question-to-question.

[16] Support services provided through Title III, Part B, include transportation, information and assistance, and a number of home-based care services. For a full list of Part B support services, see table 1.

[17] Our past work has noted the importance and difficulty of providing transportation to seniors in rural areas because alternatives to seniors' own transportation are less likely to be available and special transportation services are limited. GAO, *Transportation-Disadvantaged Seniors: Efforts to Enhance Senior Mobility Could Benefit from Additional Guidance and Information*, GAO-04-971 (Washington D.C.: August 2004).

[18] Our past work has found that mass transit options may pose scheduling and accessibility challenges for seniors. See GAO-04-971.

[19] Agency officials' observations about seniors' increased interest in home-delivered meals are echoed by data describing trends in the use of OAA meal services. Although congregate meal programs still served more clients than home-delivered meal programs in fiscal year 2008, the Congressional Research Service found that from 1990 to 2008, the number of home-delivered meals served grew by almost 44 percent, while the number of congregate meals served declined by 34 percent. See Collelo, Kirsten J., *Older Americans Act: Title III Nutrition Services Program*, Congressional Research Service, RS21202 (November 2009).

[20] In addition to home-based services provided by OAA programs, many receive services through Medicaid. Provisions of the Patient Protection and Affordable Care Act, such as that

authorizing the Community Choice First Option, which establishes an additional Medicaid waiver, and that constituting the CLASS Act, which establishes a national voluntary insurance program, may provide additional sources of coverage for in-home care services. Pub. L. No. 111-148, §§ 2401 and §§ 8001 – 8002, 124 Stat. 297-301 and 828 – 47.

[21] See Collelo, Kirsten J., 2009.

[22] National Association of State Units on Aging, *The Economic Crisis and Its Impact on State Aging Programs: Results of All State Survey* (November 2009).

[23] Hicks, Jennifer and Eric R. Kingston, "The Economic Crisis: How Fare Older Americans?" *Generations Journal of the American Society on Aging* (Fall 2009).

[24] In our final report, we hope to estimate the numbers of individuals in need of meal, transportation and home-based care services, and to provide information on what characteristics are related to need for these services and to the likelihood that these needs are being addressed. We plan to do this by conducting regression analyses of publicly available national data on the 60 and over population.

[25] OAA allows states to transfer funds among Title III Part B support services and Title III Part C meal programs. 42 U.S.C. § 3023(c)(2). States may transfer up to 40 percent of funds among Part C meal programs, and may transfer up to 30 percent of support services funds to the meal programs and vice versa. The Assistant Secretary of Aging also can grant a waiver that allows states to transfer additional funds. Funds for Title III Part E caregiver services cannot be transferred under this authority.

[26] Fiscal year 2008 is the most recent year for which state level data are available.

[27] SUAs that administer Medicaid programs received additional Recovery Act funds. 42 U.S.C. § 3023(c)(2). State officials in Wisconsin said although the funds were not specifically for OAA programs, they did help maintain some SUA program operations.

## Chapter 4

# TESTIMONY OF PAUL DOWNEY, PRESIDENT, NATIONAL ASSOCIATION OF NUTRITION AND AGING SERVICED PROGRAM (NANASP), BEFORE THE SENATE SPECIAL COMMITTEE ON AGING HEARING, "2011 REAUTHORIZATION OF THE OLDER AMERICANS ACT"

Senator Udall:

It is my pleasure to testify today at this important hearing. I commend your interest in wanting to improve the Older Americans Act, particularly the nutrition program. It is also a pleasure to participate with our nation's outstanding Assistant Secretary for Aging, Kathy Greenlee.

I come today wearing two hats. I am President of the National Association of Nutrition and Aging Services Programs -- NANASP. I am also President and CEO of Senior Community Centers of San Diego with 15 years in the Older Americans Act aging network.

You have a particular interest in programs and activities which promote wellness and foster disease prevention among older Americans. That is precisely what we are doing in San Diego.

Senior Community Centers serves 1,700 meals a day, 365 days per year to predominately low-income seniors, many of whom live on less than $200 after rent. The link between nutritious meals, health, independence and, frankly, their ability to simply survive is undeniable.

This year, in a unique partnership with visionary philanthropists, private and public partnership and collaborations with more than 25 community agencies, we opened the Gary and Mary West Senior Wellness Center. We firmly believe that it represents a model that can be replicated throughout the country – in both rural and urban settings.

Our congregate meal numbers at the Gary and Mary West Senior Wellness Center have increased each month – to almost 700 meals daily. Nutrition is the core service around which we provide case management, life-long learning and civic engagement. We then leverage our community partnerships to provide an array of additional services – at no cost to us or our clients. Our partners include Sharp Healthcare, the largest healthcare provider in San Diego County, and the College of Health and Human Services at San Diego State University. About 30 SDSU students representing five different disciplines – social work, gerontology, nursing, public health, and speech and language -- and their professors are outstationed at the Wellness Center. Our seniors receive more services, students learn about working with the elderly and professors have research opportunities.

This is what Older Americans Act dollars were intended to do -- leverage other resources beyond merely providing a meal at locations where seniors gather each day. The next reauthorization must strengthen our ability -- at the local level – to do this kind of leveraging. This can be accomplished by letting those in the aging network closest to the senior determine what is best in each of our communities.

Let me be more specific. The nutrition program must continue its requirement that meals meet RDA requirements -- especially since 73 percent of participants are at high nutritional risk; 62 percent of homebound seniors receive half or more of their daily food intake from the meal.

However, how this is achieved needs more flexibility. We anticipate a doubling of our minority elderly population in less than 20 years. To keep nutrition programs relevant to them, we must offer food choices that reflect greater cultural sensitivity.

We have boomers in our programs and more will follow. They need different menu options and approaches to serving meals to keep these programs relevant.

One modification we could make to benefit all participants is to allow greater use of fresh foods and vegetables. We have too many obstacles in too many places now keeping that from happening. As you can imagine, the interpretation of what can be accepted varies significantly from state to state and even county to county. I encountered this first-hand recently when I tried to accept a reoccurring donation of fresh fish from a sports fishing consortium. State and local regulations – which the Older Americans Act says we must comply with -- created such onerous impediments that we had to decline the fish. We must have a system where laws at all levels of government work together – consistently and fairly -- to encourage donations of fresh food and vegetables.

My NANASP views parallel my local views. We support greater flexibility at the local level on whether more funds are provided to congregate or home delivered meals.

For nutrition programs to deliver the outcomes they do, they must be adequately funded. That does not always mean more money. In this case it is about making sure that dollars intended for nutrition stay in nutrition. Today nearly $40 million in funds from the congregate nutrition program go into non-nutrition programs within the Older Americans Act. There may have been a need for that before but we don't believe there still is when we have rising demand in our programs.

We appreciate your support of the 2009 stimulus bill which provided an urgently needed $100 million in funds for the nutrition programs. Our programs faced rising food and energy costs and loss of volunteers. These funds helped avert disaster -- but the need remains and we need to see funding levels for FY 2011 as close to this level as possible.

NANASP also supports strengthening the Disease prevention and Health Promotion program in the Older Americans Act going forward. We call for Congress to either transfer this program outright into the nutrition program or set aside funding for evidence based nutrition programs which help in prevention and promotion.

Finally and with special recognition to our rural seniors, we must bolster funding for transportation services which are so essential to the nutrition programs.

NANASP has enjoyed working with the Administration on Aging in the early stages of the reauthorization process and looks forward to working especially with you Senator Udall and your colleagues on the Special Committee on Aging to achieve a successful, innovative and forward moving Older Americans Act.

## Chapter 5

# TESTIMONY OF KATHY GREENLE, ASSISTANT SECRETARY FOR AGING, U.S. DEPARTMENT OF HEALTH AND HUMAN SERVICES, BEFORE THE SENATE SPECIAL COMMITTEE ON AGING HEARING, "2011 REAUTHORIZATION OF THE OLDER AMERICANS ACT"

Thank you, Chairman Kohl, for the opportunity to testify before the Senate Special Committee on Aging at this hearing on the upcoming reauthorization of the Older Americans Act (the Act). I am pleased to discuss our efforts to solicit input from throughout the country, and to hear Wisconsin's perspectives on this important legislation that provides vital home and community-based services to older adults and their caregivers.

At the outset, I would like to commend you, Senator, for your leadership as Chairman of the Senate Special Committee on Aging, and as a member of the Senate Appropriations and Judiciary Committees whose jurisdictions impact many of the Older Americans Act programs administered by the Administration on Aging (AoA). We are grateful for the support you have provided to the Older Americans Act programs and especially for your strong interest in older workers and elder rights/consumer protection.

This is my first visit to Wisconsin since I was sworn in as Assistant Secretary over a year ago; however, I trust it will not be my last. I am impressed by the level of commitment and dedication of Wisconsin's aging network and by the interest and enthusiasm of your older citizens and their families. I would like to recognize Donna McDowell, Bureau Director, Wisconsin Aging and Disabilities Resource Bureau, as well as the Coalition of Wisconsin Aging Groups and other advocates for seniors in Wisconsin. I commend them all for their continued work on behalf of older citizens of your beautiful State. Wisconsin is a leader in so many areas related to the health and well-being of seniors, and the rest of our nation has much to learn from your citizens.

On July 14, 1965, President Johnson signed the Older Americans Act into law. Sixteen days later, on July 30, he signed legislation creating Medicare and Medicaid. These three programs, along with Social Security enacted in 1935, have served as the foundation for economic, health and social support for millions of seniors, individuals with disabilities and their families. Because of these programs, millions of older Americans have lived more secure, healthier and meaningful lives. The Older Americans Act has quietly but effectively provided nutrition and community support to millions of people across Wisconsin and across the nation. It has also protected the rights of seniors, and in many cases, has been the key to their independence.

In 1965, there were about 26 million Americans age 60 and over. Today, there are 57 million older Americans 60 and over, with many more on the immediate horizon.[1] Our senior population is not only growing larger, but becoming more diverse. The older population aged 85 and over is also projected to increase significantly. In 1990, there were 3.1 million persons 85 and over; in 2020, this figure is projected to more than double to 6.6 million persons.[2] Many will need long-term care, both in the community and when that becomes impossible, in nursing homes and other facilities. Reliance on family members, who currently provide 80 percent of the long-term care assistance for our nation's seniors, will increase.

The historic enactment of the Affordable Care Act (ACA) by President Obama on March 23, 2010 provides us with another tremendous opportunity to harness the successes and progress of the last four decades to further improve the health and lives of older Americans and support their caregivers. As you know, the ACA represents the biggest change in our national health care delivery system since 1965. And just as they were in 1965, the programs of the Older Americans Act - and our national aging network of State, tribal and community-based organizations, service providers, volunteers and family caregivers - will be called upon to complement, support and enhance these changes. How successfully we weave these multiple responsibilities together will say much for how we will care for seniors in the future.

I would like to thank you, Chairman Kohl, for your leadership in ensuring inclusion of the Elder Justice Act in the Affordable Care Act. This is landmark legislation that takes an important step in addressing the growing crisis of elder abuse.

As part of the process for reauthorizing the Older Americans Act (now authorized through FY 2011), early this year the Administration on Aging sought input from all interested parties, and offered a wide range of input options. Specifically AoA:

- Sponsored three on-site listening forums (Washington DC - February 25, 2010; Dallas - February 26, 2010; and San Francisco - March 3, 2010);
- Co-led the first of its kind listening webinar with Department of Labor (DoL) Assistant Secretary for Employment and Training, Jane Oates, to focus on
- Encouraged the conduct of State/local listening events throughout the country with receipt of on-line summaries of the events; and
- Provided online and downloadable individual input forms on its reauthorization website.

Over 400 individuals from 48 States and Territories have participated in the public input process to date, including 310 who attended one of the three on-site listening forums. A total of 264 individuals have provided written, oral or online input, or panel presentations. In addition, 12 State or local input events sponsored by six different agencies have been conducted. We believe the individuals and organizations that provided input represented the interests and concerns of thousands of consumers throughout the country. I am pleased to report that Wisconsin was an active participant in this processwith comments offered on providing information and assistance to clients of all ages; as well as strengthening and funding for advocacy activities, home modification equipment, disease prevention/health promotion activities and legal services.

The recommendations of the national organizations focused on providing/promoting:

- Single access points for long-term care information and services, evidence-based health promotion and disease prevention activities, and enhanced nursing home diversion/community living programs;
- Person-centered (self-directed) services;
- State/area flexibility to direct nutrition funding where most needed (i.e., consolidation of funding for congregate and home-delivered nutrition services funding);
- Integration of medical and human services-based long-term services and supports (LTSS), particularly in order to promote the aging network's role in health, wellness (both physical and behavioral health) and care management;
- Workforce development, utilization of technology and application of business models; and
- Increased capacity for Title VI Native American aging programs.

Overall, the types of input we received throughout the country can be grouped into two general categories-structure/administration; and service delivery and expansion.

Specifically, we are hearing the following recurring themes:

- The importance of the original Declaration of Objectives in Title I of the Older American Act that establish the guiding principles and goals of the Act in creating a society that enhances the lives of older individuals.
- The importance of the role of advocacy of the assistant secretary in coordinating and advocating on behalf of older individuals and aging issues within and across Federal agencies and departments. Also, the role of AoA and the entire aging network in advocating on behalf of older persons at the Federal, State, tribal and local levels was highlighted (Title II).
- The importance of home and community-based services and the aging network infrastructure for responding to the needs and preferences of older individuals to remain, when possible, in their homes and communities (Title III).
- The importance of Information and Assistance and the need for consolidated access, such as Single Entry Points or Aging and Disability Resource Centers (ADRCs) -- first created here in Wisconsin in 1998.

- The need for flexibility in programming to respond to local and area needs – often mentioned in the context of consolidating congregate and home-delivered meals into one nutrition services allocation and program without prescribed levels of funding for each category from the Federal level.
- The need to include a broader range of evidence-based interventions as a component of Health Promotion, Disease Prevention.
- The need for greater inclusiveness of various types of kinship care and more respite services in the provision of caregiver services.
- The unique challenges of providing services and meeting the needs of individuals residing in rural, remote and frontier areas of the country.
- The importance of innovation, research, demonstrations and training authority and funding and how it has played a significant role in building and enhancing the field of aging. (Title IV)
- The strong encouragement for active collaboration between AoA and DoL to reinforce the dual purpose of the Older American Community Service Employment Program to offer community service opportunities while providing training and employment for low-income seniors (Title V).
- The need to fully recognize the sovereignty of tribal nations in Title VI and to consolidate programming for Tribes from other parts of the Act to Title VI. Also, comments were made to achieve greater parity with Title III.
- The importance of focusing on elder rights and elder justice issues and to look broadly at building an effective infrastructure through enhanced coordination with domestic violence, adult protective services, ombudsman, and consumer protection organizations and entities (Title VII).

Within the Administration, the process for the reauthorization has also begun. We are discussing the input we have received within the Department of Health and Human Services.

For the past 45 years, the Older Americans Act has become recognized and highly regarded for stimulating the development of a comprehensive home and community-based supportive services system that has enhanced the lives of older individuals and their family caregivers. We look forward to the reauthorization process as a means to strengthen and position this important piece of legislation so that its programs and services will continue to carry out the important mission of helping elderly individuals maintain their health and independence in their homes and communities.

Thank you. I would be happy to answer any questions.

In: The Older Americans Act: Provisions,... ISBN: 978-1-61122-801-4
Editor: Jamie N. Palamino ©2011 Nova Science Publishers, Inc.

*Chapter 6*

# OLDER AMERICANS ACT: LONG-TERM CARE OMBUDSMAN PROGRAM

*Kirsten J. Colello*

## SUMMARY

The purpose of the Long-Term Care Ombudsman Program is to investigate and resolve complaints made by, or on behalf of, older persons who are residents of long-term care facilities. Established under Title VII of the Older Americans Act (OAA), the Administration on Aging (AoA) within the Department of Health and Human Services (HHS) administers the nationwide program. As of 2007, there are 53 state Long-Term Care Ombudsman Programs operating in all 50 states, the District of Columbia, Guam, and Puerto Rico, and 569 local programs. The program is funded by two separate titles of the OAA, in addition to other federal sources, state funds, and nonfederal funds. With respect to staffing, the program receives significant support from volunteers. In FY2007, over 1,300 paid staff and 12,600 volunteers investigated more than 282,000 resident complaints. Issues regarding residents' care were the chief complaint in nursing homes, followed by residents' rights issues in FY2007. Among residents in other long-term care facilities, the top complaint categories were quality of life and residents' rights.

An evaluation conducted by the Institute of Medicine (IOM) in 1995 concluded that the program is understaffed and underfunded to carry out its broad and complex responsibilities. In March 1999, HHS's OIG recommended that AoA work with states to strengthen the program by developing guidelines for a minimum level of program visibility that include criteria for the frequency and length of regular visits, as well as the ratio of ombudsman program staff to longterm care beds; further developing strategies for recruiting, training, and supervising more volunteers; and establishing ways in which ombudsman programs can enhance collaboration with the state nursing home survey and certification agencies, which are responsible for oversight of nursing home care quality. This report will be updated occasionally.

## BACKGROUND

The purpose of the Long-Term Care Ombudsman Program is to respond to the needs of residents facing problems in long-term care facilities, including nursing homes, assisted living facilities, board and care homes, and other similar adult residential care settings. Ombudsmen are available to help all long-term care facility residents, not only those residents in facilities certified by Medicare and/or Medicaid. Created in 1972 as a Public Health Service (PHS) demonstration project in five states, authority for administering the ombudsman demonstration program was transferred to the Administration on Aging (AoA) within the Department of Health and Human Services (HHS) in 1974. The results of the demonstration effort led to statutory authority under the Older Americans Act (OAA)[1] in 1978 (P.L. 95-478). In 1987, the program was given a separate authorization of appropriations (P.L. 100-175) and, in 1992, the program was incorporated into a new Title VII of the Act authorizing vulnerable elder rights protection activities (P.L. 102-375). Also in 1992, a provision was added to the OAA amendments requiring AoA to establish a permanent National Ombudsman Resource Center. The most recent amendments to the OAA in 2006 (P.L. 109-365) made no major changes to the program.

There are 53 state Long-Term Care Ombudsman Programs operating in all 50 states, the District of Columbia, Guam, and Puerto Rico, and 569 local programs as of 2007.[2] The AoA's National Ombudsman Reporting System (NORS) compiles national statistics relating to ombudsman activities. This information includes number, status, and type of cases reported to state and local ombudsman programs; data on staff, volunteers, and funding; and, other ombudsman activities.

## FUNCTION

The OAA requires State Units on Aging to establish an Office of the Long-Term Care Ombudsman. The functions of the state ombudsman programs are mandated by law and include

- identifying, investigating, and resolving resident complaints;
- protecting the legal rights of residents, advocating for systemic change, and providing information and consultation to residents and their families; and
- publicizing issues of importance to residents.

Complaints investigated by ombudsmen relate to actions, inactions, or decisions of long-term care providers or other agencies that adversely affect the health, safety, welfare, or rights of residents. Among its other responsibilities, the Office is to analyze and monitor federal, state, and local policies that affect residential long-term care facilities.

The federal law requires that a full-time ombudsman administer the program at the state level; local ombudsmen may be designated by the state and are considered to be representatives of the Office. According to AoA, most state ombudsman programs are located in State Units on Aging, but programs in 15 states and the District of Columbia[3] are located in other types of organizational settings, such as non-profit organizations. Variation exists partly because the OAA gives each state discretion in determining many aspects of the ombudsman program. For example, states can decide

- where ombudsman programs may be located organizationally within the state,
- whether enabling legislation should be passed at the state level, and
- whether additional funding will be made available through state and local sources.[4]

These differences mean that the structure, operation, and effectiveness of the ombudsman programs can vary from state to state.

In addition, ombudsman programs in 12 states are authorized or mandated under state law to advocate on behalf of consumers who receive home and community-based care. According to a 2007 report of state Home Care Ombudsman programs, the majority of these states have responsibility for complaints regarding services provided under the state's Medicaid home and community-based waivers.[5] States also reported that home care ombudsman cover complaints regarding home health agency services and home care services that may be privately funded, state funded, or funded through the OAA. In general, state Home Care Ombudsman programs are supported by state general funds.

## AUTHORIZATION AND FUNDING

The OAA Amendments of 2006 (P.L. 109-365) reauthorized the ombudsman program for five years through FY2011. Ombudsman services are authorized under two separate titles of the OAA:

- Title III – Grants for States and Community Programs on Aging, and
- Title VII – Vulnerable Elder Rights Protection Activities.

Title III authorizes grants to states for supportive services and senior centers that provide for a wide range of social services, including long-term care ombudsman services. Title VII has two separate authorizations for support of ombudsman activities: Chapter 2 (the long-term care ombudsman program) and Chapter 3 (the elder abuse prevention program).[6]

While the majority of federal funding for ombudsman activities comes from appropriations for Titles III and VII of the OAA, the program also receives substantial non-federal support. **Table 1** shows total support for ombudsman activities in FY2007. Total FY2007 funding for ombudsman activities from all sources combined (federal and non-federal) was $81.8 million. Of that total, 58.8% represented funding from federal sources, with 32.2% from Title III funds, 20.8% from Title VII funds, and 5.9% from other federal funds. In FY2007, nonfederal funding represented 41.2% of total support (32.7% state funding and 8.5% local funding).

## Table 1. Long-Term Care Ombudsman Program Funding, by Source FY2007

| Total FY2007 funds (in millions) | | | $81.8 | 100% |
|---|---|---|---|---|
| Federal funds | Total | | $48.1 | 58.8% |
| | Title III, OAA | | $26.3 | 32.2% |
| | Title VII, OAA | Chapter 2: ombudsman program | $14.7 | 18.0% |
| | | Chapter 3: elder abuse prevention | $2.3 | 2.8% |
| | Other | | $4.8 | 5.9% |
| State funds | | | $26.7 | 32.7% |
| Local funds | | | $7.0 | 8.5% |

Source: CRS analysis based on AoA, *2007 National Ombudsman Reporting System Data Tables*: Table A-9 Long- Term Care Ombudsman Program Funding.

Note: Data may not sum to totals due to rounding.

From FY2000 through FY2007, the share of federal funding for Long-Term Care Ombudsman Program activities remained relatively constant, while the proportion of state funding increased from 27.6% to 32.7% and spending at the local level decreased from 13.4% to 8.5%.

## STAFFING

In FY2007, there were approximately 1,311 paid staff (full-time equivalents) in state Long-Term Care Ombudsman Programs, an increase of 35% since FY2000.[7] Despite this increase, the program still relies heavily on volunteers to carry out program responsibilities. Nine out of every ten ombudsman staff serve as volunteers. In FY2007, there were over 12,600 total volunteers, 8,668 of which were certified to investigate complaints. While the number of paid ombudsman staff has increased from FY2000, the total number of volunteers decreased 7% during this same time period (from just over 13,600 in FY2000). A nationwide study conducted by the National Long Term Care Ombudsman Center found that 45 state ombudsman programs have volunteer programs and 37 state programs reported having a certification process for their volunteers as of 1999.[8]

The 1995 IOM evaluation along with a study done by the Office of Inspector General (OIG) in HHS (1991) acknowledged the importance of volunteers as a contributing factor to high complaint resolution rates in this program.[9] However, the IOM evaluation advised that adequate methods for recruiting, training, and supervising volunteers are essential to maximum utilization of ombudsman program volunteers. State programs have different procedures for certification of volunteers, varying from required classroom training to tests for certification. Data from AoA's NORS report that over two-thirds of volunteers (69%) were trained and certified to investigate complaints in FY2007, a 3% increase since FY2000.

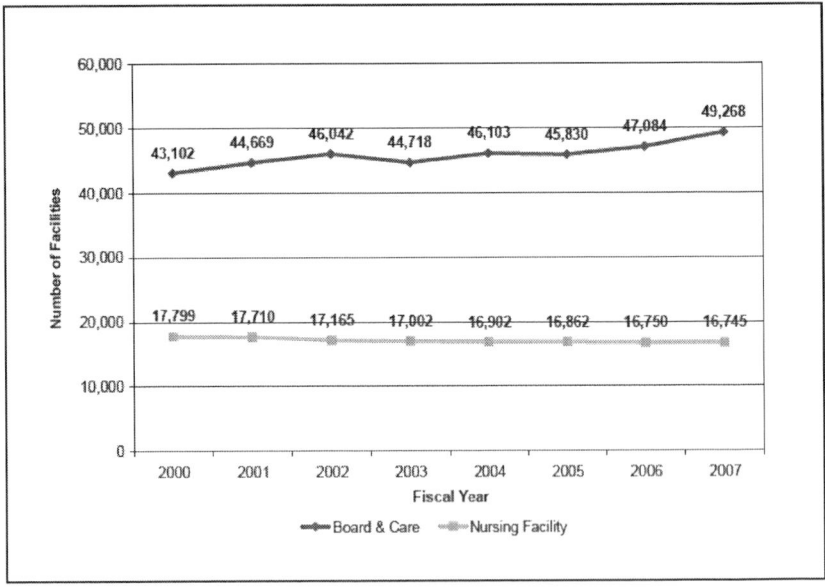

Source: CRS analysis based on AoA, *2007 National Ombudsman Reporting System Data Tables*: Table A-6-A Long- Term Care Ombudsman Program Funding.

Note: The number of nursing facilities and board and care homes and similar facilities includes those regulated (licensed or registered) in the state. Under the OAA, the ombudsman program covers all such facilities, whether regulated or unregulated by the state; however, according to the OMB instructions for completing the Long Term Care Ombudsman Program Reporting Form for NORS, it would not be possible for the program to provide the total number of unregulated facilities and beds. Therefore, the actual number of these facilities may be higher. The number of nursing homes may be slightly higher than estimates by the Centers for Medicare and Medicaid Services (CMS), which include only nursing homes certified to participate in Medicare and/or Medicaid.

Figure 1. Number of Long-Term Care Facilities, by Facility Type FY2000 to FY2007

In FY2007, ombudsmen reported just over 16,700 nursing facilities and more than 49,000 other residential long-term care facilities operating nationwide.[10] Since FY2000 the total number of regulated facilities has increased by 8% from almost 61,000 to more than 66,000 in FY2007 (see **Figure 1**). This increase is due to an increase in assisted living facilities, board and care homes, and other similar facilities, which more than offset the decrease in nursing homes over the past seven years.

## Workload

Due to the requirement that ombudsmen investigate and resolve complaints of all residents in residential long-term care facilities, the workload of staff and volunteers is substantial, as shown by the reported ratio of staff to facilities and beds. The nationwide ratio of paid ombudsman to facilities was one ombudsman to every 50 facilities in FY2007, a smaller ratio than reported in FY2000 (one ombudsman to every 62 facilities). Nationwide, there were a reported 2.8 million facility beds under the program's jurisdiction (just over 1.7 million nursing home beds and about 1.1 million beds in other long-term care facilities) in FY2007. The nationwide ratio of full-time paid ombudsman to facility beds was about one ombudsman per 2,200 beds, a smaller ratio than reported in FY2000 (one ombudsman per 2,800 beds). However, it is important to note that these ratios are nationwide, and each state has a unique ratio of paid ombudsman staff per facility bed.[11]

The 1995 IOM study recommended a standard staffing ratio of one paid full-time equivalent staff per 2,000 long-term care facility beds.

Despite the high number of facilities to be covered by each ombudsman, ombudsman staff and volunteers visited 83% of nursing homes on a regular basis (defined as at least quarterly) in FY2007. These visits were not in response to a complaint. The percentage of nursing homes visited regularly by ombudsman staff was greater than visits by staff to other residential longterm care facilities. The proportion of regular visits to assisted living and other long-term care facilities was 47% in FY2007.

## Training

State ombudsman programs are responsible for training new and existing staff. The OAA contains only basic requirements for training and stipulates that the AoA is to develop model standards for training long-term care ombudsman, both paid and unpaid volunteers. Furthermore, the law stipulates that the State Long Term Care Ombudsman is responsible for establishing procedures for training representatives of the local ombudsman program based on the AoA standards and that training is to be developed in consultation with representatives of citizen groups, long-term care providers, and ombudsmen. In the absence of specific federal training requirements and/or required training materials, many states have developed their own standards. Several states provide the training directly through an individual who is responsible for conducting all of the training while some states require local ombudsman programs to conduct training. State longterm care ombudsman programs have received assistance in developing training programs from the National Long Term Care Ombudsman Resource Center, operated by the National Citizen's Coalition for Nursing Home Reform.[12]

## PROGRAM DATA AND RESIDENT COMPLAINTS

In FY2007, AoA data show that ombudsmen opened just over 186,000 new cases of resident complaints and closed more than 184,000 cases in all types of facilities.[13] Between FY2000 and FY2007, the total number of cases closed increased by more than one-third (34%).

Since 2000, resident care issues have been the primary complaint category in nursing homes. Poor quality of care in nursing homes has been attributed to insufficient numbers of staff to care for residents. However, the relationship between staffing and quality of care is complex and includes a range of staffing-related issues such as wages and benefits, education, training, experience, and staff turnover.[14]

The top five resident complaints in nursing homes for FY2007 are

(1) unheeded requests for assistance;
(2) problems with discharge planning or eviction notification and procedures;
(3) lack of dignity or respect for residents by staff;

(4) lack of quantity, quality, variety, and choice in food; and
(5) improper handling of residents that resulted in unexplained accidents or injury.

These top five complaints have remained among the top 10 resident complaints in nursing homes since FY2000.

Similarly, the top five resident complaints in other long-term care facilities have remained the same since FY2000 and are

(1) lack of quantity, quality, variety, and choice in food,
(2) problems with medication administration or organization,
(3) inadequate discharge or eviction notice or procedure,
(4) poor equipment or building conditions, and
(5) lack of dignity or respect for residents by staff.

In FY2007, the top five resident complaints in nursing homes and other long-term care facilities accounted for one-fifth of all complaints for each facility type.

## PROGRAM EVALUATION

The most recent national evaluation of the ombudsman program, conducted in 1995 by the IOM, concluded that the program plays an important role in improving long-term care services, but is understaffed and underfunded to carry out its broad and complex responsibilities.[15] In March 1999, HHS's OIG recommended that AoA work with states to strengthen the program by: developing guidelines for a minimum level of program visibility that include criteria for the frequency and length of regular visits, as well as the ratio of ombudsman program staff to longterm care beds; further developing strategies for recruiting, training, and supervising more volunteers; and establishing ways in which ombudsman programs can enhance collaboration with the state nursing home survey and certification agencies, which are responsible for oversight of nursing home care quality.[16]

A 2000 study of state ombudsman programs reaffirmed the importance of several factors identified in the IOM evaluation as key to program effectiveness including sufficient funding, staff, and volunteers; autonomy of ombudsman program in organizational placement within the state; a supportive political or social environment; and strong interorganizational relationships.[17] A study of local ombudsman programs conducted in two states, California and New York, in 2004, found wide variation both across and within each state's program in terms of program location (area agency on aging versus nonprofit organization) and the number of paid staff versus volunteers. Despite reporting that their program budgets were inadequate to support their mandated requirements, program coordinators in both states perceived their programs as effective, more so in the nursing home setting than in board and care facilities. Program coordinators in both states similarly identified staffing, resident care, and residents' rights as the most pressing issues.[18]

## End Notes

[1] Congress in 1978 amended the OAA (P.L. 95-478) to include a requirement that each state develop a Long-Term Care Ombudsman Program in order to protect the health, safety, welfare, quality of care, and rights of the institutionalized residents in nursing facilities, board and care homes, assisted living facilities, and other similar facilities. For further information, see CRS Report RL3 1336, *The Older Americans Act: Programs, Funding, and 2006 Reauthorization (P.L. 109-365)*, by Carol O'Shaughnessy and Angela Napili.

[2] Guam's ombudsman program is for all elderly, not just those residing in long-term care facilities.

[3] Based on CRS discussions with Sue Wheaton, Ombudsman Program Specialist, Administration on Aging, as of November 2006, programs in Alaska, Colorado, Connecticut, District of Columbia, Kansas, Kentucky, New Hampshire, New Jersey, Maine, Oregon, Rhode Island, Virginia, Vermont, Washington, Wisconsin, and Wyoming are either free-standing programs or located in private, non-profit agencies or a larger government ombudsman program.

[4] For further information, see J. Harris-Wehling, J. Feasley, and C. Estes, eds., *Real People Real Problems: An Evaluation of the Long-Term Care Ombudsman Programs of the Older American Act*, Washington, DC: Institute of Medicine (IOM), 1995.

[5] M. Miller, *Home Care Ombudsman Programs Status Report: 2007*, National Association of State Units on Aging, November 2007.

[6] Under Chapter 3, states may use funds to support the Long-Term Care Ombudsman Program if they choose.

[7] For further information, see 2007 National Ombudsman Reporting System Data Tables, at http://www.aoa.gov/ AoARoot/AoA_Programs/Elder_Rights/Ombudsman/National_State _Data/2007/Index.aspx.

[8] G. McInnes and A. Hedt, *Volunteers in the Long Term Care Ombudsman Program: Training, Certification and Liability Coverage*, Washington, DC: National Long Term Care Ombudsman Resource Center, December 1999.

[9] For further information, see Office of Inspector General (OIG) Report OEI-02-90-02 120, *Successful Ombudsman Programs*; OEI-02-90-02121, *Ombudsman Output Measures*; and, OEI-02-90-02122, *Effective Ombudsman Programs: Six Case Studies;* J. Harris-Wehling, J. Feasley, and C. Estes, eds., Real People Real Problems: An Evaluation of the Long-Term

Care Ombudsman Programs of the Older American Act, Washington, DC: Institute of Medicine (IOM), 1995.

[10] Other residential long-term care facilities include board and care homes and similar facilities, such as residential care facilities, adult congregate living facilities, assisted living facilities, foster care homes, and other adult care homes similar to a nursing facility or board and care home that provides room, board, and personal care services to a primarily older residential population.

[11] For further information, see *2006 National Ombudsman Reporting System Data Tables*, at http://www.aoa.gov/prof/aoaprog/elder_rights/LTCombudsman/National_and_State_Data/2006nors/2006tables.xls, visited April 11, 2008.

[12] For further information on training materials to assist states, see the National Ombudsman Resource Center website at http://www.ltcombudsman.org/.

[13] According to the NORS Reporting Requirements Form (OMB No. 0985-0005), a complaint is a concern brought to, or initiated by, the ombudsman for investigation and action by or on behalf of one or more residents of a long-term care facility relating to health, safety, welfare, or rights of a resident. Each inquiry involving one or more complaints constitutes an "opened" case, which then requires ombudsman investigation, strategy to resolve, and follow-up. A case is reported "closed" when none of the complaints within the case require any further action on the part of the ombudsman and every complaint has been assigned the appropriate disposition code.

[14] J. Schnelle et al., *Relationship of Nursing Home Staffing to Quality of Care*. Health Services Research, 39(2): 225- 250, April 2004; R. Kane. *Commentary: Nursing Home Staffing—More Is Necessary but Not Necessarily Sufficient*, 39(2): 251-256, April 2004.

[15] J. Harris-Wehling, J. Feasley, and C. Estes, eds., *Real People Real Problems: An Evaluation of the Long-Term Care Ombudsman Programs of the Older American Act*, Washington, DC: Institute of Medicine (IOM), 1995.

[16] OIG Report OEI-02-98-00351, *Long-Term Care Ombudsman Program: Overall Capacity*.

[17] C. Estes, et al. *State Long Term Care Ombudsman Programs: Factors Associated with Perceived Effectiveness*, The Gerontologist, vol. 44(1), pp.104-115, 2004.

[18] C. Estes, *Enhancing the Performance of Local Long Term Care Ombudsman in New York Sate and California: Chartbook*, University of California, San Francisco, 2006.

# CHAPTER SOURCES

The following chapters were previously published:

Chapter 1 – This is an edited reformatted and augmented version of a Congressional Research Service publication, report RL33880, dated April 9, 2010.

Chapter 2 – This is an edited reformatted and augmented version of a Congressional Research Service publication, report RS21202, dated February 1, 2010.

Chapter 3 – This is an edited reformatted and augmented version of a United States Government Accountability Office publication, report GAO-10-1024T, dated September 7, 2010.

Chapter 4 – These remarks were delivered as testimony. Paul Downey, President, National Association of Nutrition and Aging Services Programs, before Senate Special Committee on Aging Hearing-2011 Reauthorization of the Older Americans Act.

Chapter 5 – These remarks were delivered as testimony given on September 7, 2010. Kathy Greenlee, Assistant Secretary for Aging, United States Department of Health and Human Services, before the Senate Special Committee on Aging Field Hearing on Reauthorization of the Older Americans Act.

Chapter 6 – This is an edited reformatted and augmented version of a Congressional Research Service publication, report RS21297, dated July 1, 2009.

# INDEX

## A

abuse, vii, 1, 3, 6, 14, 18, 23, 25, 29, 30, 71, 78, 79
accessibility, 62
accounting, viii, 35, 36
administrators, 50
advocacy, 71, 72
agencies, vii, 6, 10, 15, 26, 27, 28, 29, 31, 35, 36, 39, 47, 48, 49, 50, 52, 53, 54, 55, 56, 57, 58, 59, 60, 61, 62, 66, 71, 72, 76, 77, 83, 84
aging society, 61
Alaska, 43, 84
American Recovery and Reinvestment Act, 1, 4, 5, 9, 20, 21, 31, 32, 39, 48, 49, 60
appointments, 10
appropriations, vii, viii, 1, 3, 5, 6, 15, 16, 19, 20, 22, 24, 28, 29, 33, 36, 39, 76, 78
assessment, 37, 42, 44
autonomy, 83

## B

barriers, 53
basic needs, 49
budget deficit, 58
business model, 72

## C

caregivers, viii, 2, 4, 10, 15, 23, 24, 29, 37, 47, 49, 51, 52, 54, 69, 70, 73
caregiving, 6, 10, 20, 24, 38, 45, 54
Census, 54, 62
certification, 76, 79, 80, 83
chronic diseases, 55
churches, vii, 1, 3, 9
class, 32
classroom, 80
clients, 48, 54, 55, 62, 66, 71
climate, 60
commodity, 21, 25, 38
community, vii, 1, 3, 6, 7, 9, 11, 12, 15, 26, 27, 28, 29, 30, 37, 49, 51, 53, 60, 61, 62, 66, 69, 70, 71, 72, 73, 78
community service, vii, 1, 3, 11, 12, 26, 28, 29, 30, 73
community support, 70
community-based organizations, 6, 71
community-based services, 7, 37, 49, 51, 53, 61, 69, 72
competition, 30
compilation, 31
complaints, viii, 14, 75, 77, 78, 79, 80, 81, 82, 83, 85
complement, 11, 52, 71
compliance, 42
conference, 12, 14, 22
consent, 6

Consolidated Appropriations Act, 1, 4, 7, 9, 12, 13, 14, 15, 19, 20, 21, 22
consolidation, 72
consumer protection, 70, 73
coordination, 15, 28, 51, 73
cost, 11, 30, 44, 66
cost-benefit analysis, 44
counseling, 6, 10, 12, 13, 25, 29, 37, 42, 51
covering, 61

# D

daily living, 43
data collection, 29
database, 60
demonstrations, 73
Department of Agriculture, 3, 21, 30, 32, 38
Department of Health and Human Services, viii, 3, 29, 36, 46, 47, 52, 69, 73, 75, 76
diabetes, 55
diet, 42
dignity, 59, 82, 83
directives, 33
disability, 7, 20
disaster, 67
disposition, 85
District of Columbia, viii, 7, 31, 48, 50, 51, 60, 61, 62, 75, 76, 77, 84
domestic violence, 73
donations, 53, 62, 67
donors, 10

# E

economic crisis, 9, 55
economic downturn, 9, 10, 13, 48, 49, 54
efficiency, 32
elderly population, 44, 66
elders, 13
emergency response, 52
employment, vii, 1, 3, 11, 12, 28, 29, 30, 73
encouragement, 73

equipment, 42, 71, 83
examinations, 12
expenditures, 58, 61
exploitation, vii, 1, 3, 14, 25, 29, 30

# F

family members, 38, 70
federal funds, 43, 60, 78
federal law, 28, 77
federal programs, 26, 29
fishing, 67
flexibility, 20, 28, 48, 53, 56, 57, 66, 67, 72, 73
food intake, 43, 66
formula, 30, 39
fraud, 6

# G

gerontology, 66
grant programs, 26, 28
growth factor, 39
guidelines, 32, 76, 83
guiding principles, 72

# H

health care reform, 2, 8, 53
health education, 29
home care services, 13, 43, 63, 78
home value, 55
hospitalization, 48, 55
housing, vii, 1, 3, 9, 37

# I

impacts, 44
independence, 7, 50, 59, 66, 70, 74
Independence, 7, 10, 17, 20, 23, 25
Indians, 28

inflation, 32, 40
infrastructure, 72, 73
insecurity, viii, 35, 36, 44
isolation, 9

## J

job creation, 26
Judiciary Committee, 69
jurisdiction, 81

## K

Kentucky, 84

## L

language barrier, 53
layoffs, 58
leadership, 69, 71
learning, 66
legislation, vii, 1, 3, 5, 19, 26, 27, 28, 39, 44, 53, 69, 70, 71, 73, 77
local government, 10, 58
long-term services, 72
long-term services and supports, 72
long-term services and supports (LTSS), 72

## M

Maine, 84
majority, 78
malnutrition, 55
management, 7, 8, 11, 13, 51, 66, 72
Medicaid, viii, 6, 7, 8, 11, 20, 29, 44, 47, 53, 62, 63, 70, 76, 78, 80
Medicare, viii, 2, 6, 8, 11, 19, 20, 31, 47, 53, 62, 70, 76, 80
Medicare Modernization Act, 11
medication, 83
methodology, 50

Miami, 53, 62
minimum wage, 12
minority groups, 44
modification, 67, 71
monitoring, 58
Montana, 45, 52

## N

National Survey, 43, 45
Native Americans, vii, 1, 4, 13, 17, 18, 21, 23, 25, 29
neglect, vii, 1, 3, 14, 25, 29, 30
nursing, ix, 7, 14, 20, 54, 66, 70, 72, 75, 76, 80, 81, 82, 83, 84, 85
nursing home, ix, 7, 20, 54, 70, 72, 75, 76, 80, 81, 82, 83, 84
nutrients, 44
nutrition, vii, 1, 3, 4, 9, 10, 13, 18, 21, 23, 25, 26, 28, 32, 33, 35, 36, 37, 38, 39, 40, 41, 42, 43, 44, 45, 46, 48, 49, 51, 55, 58, 59, 65, 66, 67, 70, 72, 73
nutrition programs, 1, 4, 38, 39, 59, 66, 67

## O

Obama Administration, 20
obstacles, 67
Oklahoma, 45
Omnibus Appropriations Act,, 2, 4, 12, 19
opportunities, 11, 13, 25, 27, 37, 66, 73
outreach, 2, 8, 11, 13, 29, 48, 55
overhead costs, 58
oversight, 76, 83

## P

parallel, 67
parity, 73
performance, 13, 30, 50
permission, iv

personal communication, 45
persons with disabilities, 7, 29, 37
physical activity, 7
pleasure, 65
population group, 29, 54
poverty, 32, 44, 53
prevention, 7, 9, 14, 17, 18, 20, 23, 25, 29, 30, 31, 36, 40, 44, 65, 67, 71, 72, 78, 79
procurement, 38
profit, 13, 29, 77, 84
program administration, 6
programming, 73
project, 42, 76
public health, 66
Puerto Rico, viii, 43, 62, 75, 76
purchasing power, 40

## Q

quality assurance, 8
quality of life, ix, 76
quality standards, 42

## R

real terms, 40
recession, 12, 55
recognition, 26, 67
recommendations, iv, 14, 26, 44, 71
recruiting, 76, 80, 83
recycling, 11
regression, 63
reliability, 61
rent, 66
replication, 8
research and development, 26
resolution, 79
resources, 6, 12, 27, 49, 52, 54, 59, 60, 61, 66
retirement, 6, 10, 32, 55
rights, ix, 4, 18, 23, 25, 29, 70, 73, 76, 77, 84, 85
rural areas, 37, 42, 55, 62

## S

sample survey, 60
scheduling, 62
screening, 37, 42, 48, 55
sedentary behavior, 36
Senate, 6, 9, 27, 32, 33, 65, 69
sensitivity, 66
service provider, 27, 37, 42, 49, 50, 52, 71
social environment, 84
Social Security, 70
social services, 3, 26, 27, 28, 40, 78
social support, 70
socialization, viii, 35, 36, 43, 44
sovereignty, 73
speech, 66
staffing, ix, 75, 81, 82, 84
State Department, 8
statistics, 77
stimulus, 12, 67
streams, 57
stretching, 58
support services, 2, 6, 10, 13, 14, 24, 50, 53, 54, 56, 58, 62, 63
surplus, 28
survey, 43, 44, 48, 50, 53, 54, 55, 56, 57, 58, 59, 60, 62, 76, 83
systemic change, 77

## T

technical assistance, 6, 10
testing, 8, 60
time frame, 29
Title IV, 4, 7, 8, 10, 11, 17, 20, 21, 23, 24, 25, 30, 32, 73
training, vii, 1, 4, 6, 8, 10, 12, 13, 20, 26, 27, 30, 51, 73, 76, 80, 82, 83, 85
training programs, 27, 82
transparency, 33

transportation, viii, 10, 12, 13, 47, 48, 49, 51, 53, 54, 55, 57, 62, 63, 67

## U

USDA, 3, 25, 38, 39, 40, 45

## V

vegetables, 67
victims, 28
vitamins, 42

## W

wages, 12, 82
waiver, 63
web, 60
welfare, 26, 77, 84, 85
wellness, 8, 31, 65, 72
White House, 3, 10, 14, 16, 17, 18, 19, 22, 26, 29, 32, 33
workers, 12, 26, 70
workload, 81